TABLE OF CONTENTS

INTRODUCTION

This book is for everyday Americans.

In other words, it's not for lawyers.

The law is confusing. Even lawyers, who are trained in the law, have trouble understanding it. But I believe the law should be accessible to non-lawyers, especially when that law is the guiding document of our republic.

Why does it matter who I wrote it for? Because the United States of America was designed to be governed by the people. By you. Unfortunately, Americans today take that privilege of self-government for granted. Many of us have lost sight of the fact that self-government is a privilege that is almost unheard of in human history. We have forgotten that we live in the most successful constitutional republic ever to exist.

Here's the reality: if you want to participate in governing this country, you must reach out and take hold of that opportunity.

This book is your way to do so.

In today's America, many discussions about the Constitution focus on America's failures and missteps in order to frame certain societal groups as worthy and others as unworthy. Nowhere is this dangerous trend more rampant than in the law, which is constantly revised to accomplish particular social or political goals. This book does none of that. Its only goal is to give you the knowledge you need to participate in governing this great country.

I implore you not to take this material lightly. Your understanding of it is directly tied to your ability to have a family, work in your job of choice, educate your children as you see fit, worship as you believe, and much more. You owe it to yourselves and your country to know it.

CHAPTER 1:
THE DECLARATION OF INDEPENDEN CE

"The Declaration of Independence is the ring-bolt to the chain of your nation's destiny; so, indeed, I regard it. The principles contained in that instrument are saving principles. Stand by those principles, be true to them on all occasions, in all places, against all foes, and at whatever cost."
Frederick Douglass

I know, it's a book about the Constitution.

But we have to start with the Declaration of Independence because it establishes the concepts that are the bedrock of the American republic.

We've all heard the famous line: "We hold these truths to be self-evident, that all men are created equal, that they are endowed by their Creator with certain unalienable Rights, that among these are Life, Liberty and the pursuit of Happiness." This very well may be the most powerful and beautiful declaration of individual liberty in human history. It continues: "That to secure these rights, Governments are instituted among Men, deriving their just powers from the consent of the governed." Together, these two sentences are the core of the American experiment.

Here are the five key concepts you need to understand from the Declaration of Independence:

First, **individual liberty**. The framers weren't declaring independence in order to usher in a perfect, utopian future that would somehow emerge once they overthrew British power. Unlike their counterparts in the French Revolution, they knew utopia wasn't going to happen. They also weren't focused on *group* rights like the French Revolutionaries were; they cared about securing liberty for the *individual* so that each person would be free to pursue their version of the good life. As we will see later on, the Constitution continued this focus.

3

Second, **equality before the law**. The framers' statement that "all men are created equal" is one of the most powerful sentences in history. It has inspired millions from around the globe to seek a better, freer life in the United States of America. The framers drew this concept of equality from their largely Protestant Christian religious background. That faith tradition is built on the concept of *moral equality before God*, so it wasn't too much of a leap for the framers to apply that concept to government and come up with *legal equality before the law*. The fact that we are all equal before the law does not mean that we are literally the same as everyone else. It does not mean, for instance, that differences in wealth or education are inherently wrong. Rather, it means that we are equal in our possession and pursuit of freedom.

Third, the **pursuit** of happiness. Not happiness – the *pursuit* of it. The framers weren't trying to guarantee everyone the same results when it came to lifestyle or education or career. They only claimed that Americans should be free to *pursue* happiness, however they defined that for themselves.

Fourth, you need to understand the framers' **natural law** perspective. Natural Law is the idea that there are certain rights that exist prior to government. These are rights that every human being has just by virtue of *being* human. The framers refer to this in the Declaration as "the Laws of Nature and of Nature's God." We will see this concept of natural law in the Constitution. For instance, the right to freely exercise one's religion (see Chapter 13) is considered a natural right. It is not given to us by government. It already exists, and the government's only job is to protect it.

Fifth and finally, the framers wrote that the government's power would come from the "**consent of the governed**." In other words, no one person can rule unless we all consent to that rule. We might take this for granted, but it was a revolutionary concept in the Colonial era. Most governments at that time were run by kings who believed their power came from divine authorization. Therefore, claiming that the *people* were the primary cogs in the governmental machine was a big deal.

It is important to remember that the writers and signers of the Declaration would have been executed had they been captured. This was no light matter. But they believed strongly enough in the "consent of the governed" that they were willing to take that risk. As you'll soon see, the "consent of the governed" is everywhere in the Constitution. The American system is built on it.

How does "consent of the governed" look in real life? It looks like representative government. In other words, we govern through the representatives we elect. We don't all have to go to Washington, D.C. to make our voices heard. (If we were a pure democracy, we would have to do that, which is why it is incorrect to say that the United States is a democracy. It's not. It's a republic that is built on democratic norms.). Instead, our elected representatives do that for us. They make our voices heard. It is through our representative system that the "consent of the governed" can work.

Why not just get rid of the representatives and stick with pure majority rule? Because of human nature. Humans are flawed creatures whose passions can swing from one extreme to another. If our government were based on pure majority rule, the law would swing from one extreme to the other along with the passions of the majority. A representative government, on the other hand, means that the people and their elected representatives will need to talk about the pros and cons of every decision. The genius of the representative system is that it makes sure that decisions are based as much as possible on reason, not passion.

CHAPTER 2: BEFORE THE CONSTITUTION

I said I would keep this simple, and I mean it. However, before we get into the actual provisions of the Constitution, we have to understand three key concepts about the Constitution as a whole.

* * * * *

The first key concept is the **separation of powers**. The American governmental power is separated into three branches: legislative, executive, judicial. They can't mix, combine, or trade responsibilities with each other.

The legislative branch is Congress. The Congress includes the House of Representatives and the Senate. We, the American people, elect the members of Congress. Congress' job is to write the laws. No one else – not the president, not judges, not anyone else – can have that job. Why is that? Because Congress is elected. The framers wanted to make sure that those who write the laws are directly accountable to the people.

The executive branch is the President. The President's powers include the veto power, acting as Commander in Chief of the Army and Navy, granting pardons, making treaties, appointing judges, and – in general – "tak[ing] Care that the Laws be faithfully executed." That's it. Think about that for a minute. The entire country goes into a frenzy every four years about how presidential candidates are either going to save the country or ruin it, but Congress' grant of power to the executive power is actually quite limited.

The judicial branch is composed of federal judges. Their job is to neutrally apply the law to disputes about the Constitution. They are not supposed to make new laws. They are not elected, which may seem strange in a democratic republic like ours. If judges were elected, however, they would make decisions based on the political desires of the people who elected them (i.e., not neutrally). Since the whole point of the judicial branch is that they remain neutral in applying the law, we therefore don't want them to be elected.

Why does the separation of powers matter? First, because of human nature. The framers of the Constitution recognized that humans were flawed, self-interested creatures who would always try to gain power for themselves. James Madison was blunt about it: "Men are not angels." Power grabbing would be far easier if the powers of the government were all centralized in one place. Therefore, the framers separated the powers so that "ambition would counteract ambition." In this way, they created a government that worked *against itself* in order to minimize the dangers within human nature.

Second, because of history. The framers and their ancestors had experienced the unpredictable power of monarchs. They knew that the rule of law meant nothing without protections for individual liberty. They also knew from their study of the fall of Rome that a single power source was usually able to trample liberty and avoid accountability. They separated the powers of the government because history had made it clear that that was the best way to safeguard individual liberty.

Here's an example of how the separation of powers plays out in real life:

INS v. Chadha (1983)
　　　Congress passed the Immigration & Nationality Act, which allowed Congress (either the House of Representatives or the Senate) to require or stop deportations of illegal immigrants. Deportation decisions are normally made by the Executive (the President), *not* Congress.
　　　Mr. Chadha stayed in the United States beyond his visa deadline. The House of Representatives, using its power under the Act, voted to deport Mr. Chadha. Mr. Chadha argued that the Act violated the separation of powers because it allowed the Legislative Branch to do the Executive Branch's job.
　　　The Supreme Court held that the Act violated the separation of powers. One branch of government cannot invade the responsibilities of another branch.

Key Takeaway from INS v. Chadha:
(1) The separation of powers means that one branch of the federal government cannot interfere with the responsibilities of the other branches.

* * * * *

The second big concept is **federalism**. The three branches of government discussed above are the "horizontal" components of our federal government. In other words, it is how our federal government is divvied up so that power doesn't become too concentrated. But there is also a "vertical" separation of power between the federal government and the states. The states are a very important part of the American system. In fact, the states have a lot of independence from the federal government. This "vertical" separation is often referred to as "federalism": the separation of power between the federal government and the states.

More on this in Chapter 21.

* * * * *

The third big concept is the **why** of the Constitution. In other words, why did the framers feel it was necessary to create a Constitution at all? The short answer is that the system they began with – called the Articles of Confederation – wasn't working very well. It failed to protect the people from outside threats and failed to secure private property. It was a mess.

The framers realized that they had to come up with a fix. This would require doing two things: (1) strengthening the national government so that it could stop the states from abusing their powers while also (2) ensuring that the national government could be controlled by the people and their representatives. And that's when they scrapped the Articles of Confederation and wrote what we now know as the United States Constitution.

CHAPTER 3: WHAT IS IN THE CONSTITUTION?

The Constitution begins with a brief Preamble:

We the People of the United States, in Order to form a more perfect Union, establish Justice, insure domestic Tranquility, provide for the common defense, promote the general Welfare, and secure the Blessings of Liberty to ourselves and our Posterity, do ordain and establish this Constitution for the United States of America.

The Preamble says a few key things about the Constitution.

First, it reminds us that "we the people" are the source of government. This is another way of saying what the Declaration of Independence said about the "consent of the governed."

Second, it shows us that the Constitution is not aiming for perfection. The goal is to create "a *more* perfect union." This lines up with the framers' understanding that human nature was flawed and could never achieve perfection. The best we can do is work *toward* perfection.

Third, the Preamble reminds us of what the Declaration of Independence was all about: protecting individual liberty.

* * * * *

Ever wonder what exactly is *in* the Constitution? Television pundits argue about free speech and civil rights, but we don't hear about much else. Here's how it breaks down:

There are three overall parts of the Constitution: the Articles, the Bill of Rights, and the rest of the Amendments.

I. THE ARTICLES

First, the Articles. There are seven of them, and they make up the original Constitution that was ratified in 1791.

Article I. This article deals with the legislative branch, or Congress. All legislative (law-making) power resides with Congress. Article I divides Congress into a House of Representatives and a Senate. It also lays out the powers that Congress has.

9

Article II. This article deals with the executive branch, or the President. The President's job is to execute the law.

Article III. This article concerns the judicial branch, or the Courts. It establishes the U.S. Supreme Court at the top and gives Congress the power to establish lower courts. The judicial power extends to cases that involve the Constitution and the laws of the United States.

Article IV. From here on out, the articles tend to address a variety of topics. Article IV is a perfect example: it has four sections that all address different things.

Full Faith & Credit. States must respect other states' laws.

Privileges and Immunities. States cannot discriminate on the basis of state residence. So if you are an Alaskan visiting Tennessee, the Privileges & Immunities Clause ensures you will get the same treatment under the laws of Tennessee as a Tennessean would.

Admissions Clause. Congress can admit new states to the Union.

Guarantee Clause. The United States must "guarantee to every State . . . a Republican Form of Government" and protect them from invasion. This isn't referring to the Republican party of today – it is referring to the republican form of government: a government in which the people are represented by those they elect.

Article V. Article V describes how to amend the Constitution.

Article VI.

Supremacy Clause. The Constitution is the "supreme Law of the Land."

No Religious Test Clause. Elected representatives do not have to pass a religious test to serve in Congress.

Article VII. This article simply states that the Constitution will become official law when the states ratify it, which they did in 1791.

II. THE AMENDMENTS

These seven Articles made up the original Constitution. However, soon after the Constitution was ratified, many Americans began to worry that the Constitution did not do enough to protect individual rights. Some of them wanted to add a list of rights to the Constitution to solve this problem. Others opposed adding a Bill of Rights because they felt that it would provide the federal government with an unlimited way to expand its power. In the end, James Madison agreed to add a Bill of Rights to the Constitution. He did so in order to make sure that all the states supported the Constitution. If he hadn't, there may not have been a Constitution at all since many of the states would not have ratified it without a Bill of Rights.

Here are the eight amendments in the Bill of Rights.

Amendment I. The First Amendment was designed to protect the ability of Americans to speak, assemble, publish, and worship as they see fit. It has four key components:

Establishment of Religion. Congress cannot establish a national religion.

Free Exercise of Religion. Congress cannot prohibit people from freely exercising their religion.

Free Speech and Press. Congress cannot limit the ability to speak and publish freely.

Assembly and Petition. Congress cannot prohibit people from peacefully assembling or asking the government to address a problem.

Amendment II. The Second Amendment primarily protects the right to bear arms (weapons).

Amendment III. The government can't force you to house troops in your home.

Amendment IV.

Unreasonable Searches and Seizures. The government cannot search you or your property in an unreasonable manner.

Warrants. The government must have "probable cause" to get a warrant to search or arrest you. (A warrant is a legal document authorizing a search or an arrest). In other words, if the police want to get a warrant to search your car, they have to have good reason to do so.

Amendment V.

Grand Jury. Federal felony offenses must be charged by a grand jury.

Double Jeopardy. The government cannot force a person to undergo multiple trials for the same crime.

Self-Incrimination. Ever heard the phrase "plead the fifth?" That phrase refers the Fifth Amendment. It ensures that a person accused of a crime will not be forced to be a witness against himself.

Due Process. The federal government cannot deprive citizens of "life, liberty, or property, without due process of law." It does not say that the government cannot deprive you of life, liberty, or property. Rather, it says that the government cannot deprive you of those things *without* giving you due process of law.

Takings. The government cannot take your property "for public use" without paying you "just compensation." If the government wants to turn your farm into an airstrip, it has to pay you the fair value of your farm.

Amendment VI. A criminal defendant has a right to a "speedy and public trial, by an impartial jury." In addition, he also has the right to confront any witnesses against him and offer witnesses of his own. He also has a right to a lawyer.

Amendment VII. This amendment protects the right of trial by jury.

Amendment VIII. The government cannot impose "cruel and unusual punishment" on citizens or require them to pay excessively high fines.

Those are the eight amendments in the Bill of Rights. The Bill of Rights originally applied only to the federal government. The states were not bound by them. For example, the Fourth Amendment only prohibited the federal government – not the states – from unreasonably searching you or your property. However, the Supreme Court eventually applied the Bill of Rights to the states. It is a complicated concept to grasp and we will revisit it later. **For now, you just need to know that the Bill of Rights originally applied to only the federal government, but the Supreme Court eventually applied it to the states as well**.

Amendment IX. The Ninth Amendment was written to guarantee that the rights in the state constitutions would remain valid even if a national Constitution was created.

Amendment X. The federal government only has what power the Constitution gives it. *All other power* is for the states.

Amendment XI. States cannot be sued by individual citizens. You cannot sue your home state, nor can you sue any other state.

Amendment XII. This amendment lays out the process for electing the President.

Amendment XIII. Slavery is abolished in the United States.

Amendment XIV. There is a lot of information in the Fourteenth Amendment, but the key concepts are as follows:

Privileges or Immunities. States cannot make laws that inhibit the "privileges or immunities" of United States citizenship. What are the "privileges or immunities" of United States citizenship? Good question. We're not actually sure.

Due Process. States cannot deprive citizens of life, liberty, or property without due process of law. This is identical to the Due Process provision to the Fifth Amendment; the only difference is that this one applies to the *states*, while the Fifth Amendment applies to the *federal government*.

Equal Protection. States cannot deny to anyone the equal protection of the laws.

Representatives. Each state's number of representatives depends on its population.

Voting Age. Anyone over 21 years of age can vote.

Amendment XV. The right to vote cannot be denied on the basis of race, color, or previous condition of servitude.

Amendment XVI. Congress has the power to collect taxes. Yay.

Amendment XVII. Each state gets two Senators, elected every six years.

Amendment XVIII. This amendment banned the manufacture, sale, or transportation of liquor. We call this amendment "The Prohibition Amendment" because it sparked the Prohibition Era.

Amendment XIX. Women have the right to vote.

Amendment XX. This amendment deals with a variety of things – when Congress must convene, when the President's term ends, and how the Vice President becomes President if the President dies.

Amendment   XXI.   This   amendment removed the Prohibition Amendment.

Amendment XXII. The President cannot serve more than two terms.

Amendment XXIII. This amendment gave the District of Columbia electors in the Electoral College.

Amendment XXIV. The right to vote cannot be taken away because of a failure to pay taxes.

Amendment XXV. This amendment creates procedures for how to handle a situation in which the President is unable to handle the duties of his office.

Amendment XXVI. The voting age is 18 years old.

Amendment XXVII. This amendment prohibited any laws that change how much Congress members are paid.

* * * * *

So there you have it - our Constitution.

But of course, there's more to the story than that. Since the Constitution was written, there have been lots of events that have informed how we understand it. That's the point of the rest of the book: to show you how these concepts have developed throughout our history so that you can understand what they mean in your day-to-day life. We will do this by looking at stories of people whose lives brought them face-to-face with the Constitution.

CHAPTER 4: THE LEGISLATIVE POWER – THE COMMERCE CLAUSE

The Commerce Clause is part of Article I. It gives Congress the power to make laws for interstate commerce, or commerce between states. Commerce is the process of buying and selling goods.

Here's a famous case about the Commerce Clause:

Gibbons v. Ogden (1824) (*"the steamboat case"*)

Aaron Ogden was a steamboat operator who carried freight between New York and New Jersey. He was one of a few lucky operators who received a monopoly on the New York steamboat freight market from the state of New York.

Thomas Gibbons did not get a New York state monopoly, but he was granted a federal freight license. When Gibbons tried to continue carrying freight between New York and New Jersey, the state of New York fined him because he didn't have a New York state monopoly like Ogden did. Gibbons sued, arguing that his federal license overrode the state monopoly.

The Supreme Court agreed with Gibbons. In other words, Gibbons' federal license overrode the state of New York's ability to grant monopolies. This was because Congress has the power to regulate commerce between the states. Since Gibbons was conducting interstate commerce, the states could not override Congress' authority.

Key Takeaway from Gibbons v. Ogden:
(1) Congress can regulate commerce between states (known as "interstate commerce").

Congress' power under the Commerce Clause has expanded a lot since *Gibbons v. Ogden*. This change was especially rapid during the New Deal era (1930s). President Franklin D. Roosevelt created numerous programs to try to revitalize the economy after the Great Depression. The Supreme Court upheld many of these programs using a vastly expanded Commerce Clause. The next few cases show the Supreme Court's expansion of the Commerce Clause during the 1930s.

A.L.A. Schechter Poultry Corporation v. United States (1935) (*"the chickens case"*)

In the wake of the Great Depression, Congress passed the National Industrial Recovery Act (NIRA), which gave the President the authority to write codes of conduct for certain industries. Schechter Poultry Corporation was charged with violating one of these codes of conduct. In response, Schechter argued that NIRA was unconstitutional because it gave a legislative power (writing laws) to the executive branch.

16

The Supreme Court agreed – this was an unconstitutional handing of legislative power from Congress to the President. The Court noted, however, that Congress itself could write these codes under its Commerce Clause power. It could do so even though all of Schechter Poultry's business occurred within one state! This was because Schechter Poultry's activities had a "substantial effect" on interstate commerce. This decision was a significant expansion of Congress' power to regulate commerce under the Commerce Clause of Article I.

Key Takeaways from A.L.A. Schechter Poultry Corporation v. United States:
(1) In addition to giving Congress the power to regulate **inter**state commerce (commerce between states), the Commerce Clause also enables Congress to regulate **intra**state commerce (commerce within one state) that *substantially affects* **inter**state commerce.
(2) Congress cannot delegate its legislative authority to another branch of government. Remember the separation of powers? It is meaningless if the branches can trade responsibilities with each other.

National Labor Relations Board v. Jones & Laughlin Steel Corporation (1937)

Congress passed the National Labor Relations Act in 1935. Under this Act, the government charged Jones & Laughlin Steel Company with employment discrimination. Jones & Laughlin responded that the Act was unconstitutional because Congress did not have the power to write such an act under the Commerce Clause.

The Supreme Court upheld the Act because Congress has the power under the Commerce Clause to regulate activities affecting interstate commerce (even if that effect is very small). In this case, labor management disputes had the *potential* to affect interstate commerce, and that was enough to give Congress the power to regulate those disputes under the Commerce Clause.

Key Takeaway from National Labor Relations Board v. Jones & Laughlin Steel Corporation:

(1) Congress can, under the Commerce Clause, regulate activities that have the mere *potential* to affect interstate commerce.

Wickard v. Filburn (1942) (*"the farmer case"*)

Congress passed the Agricultural Adjustment Act in 1938. This Act (which was based on the misguided notion that limiting production would revitalize the economy) set limits on how much of each crop farmers could grow. Congress justified the Act by saying that it fell within Congress' power to regulate commerce under the Commerce Clause.

Ohio farmer Roscoe Filburn harvested 12 acres' worth of wheat *above* the amount that he was allowed to harvest under the Act. He harvested this extra amount to feed his personal farm animals, not to sell in interstate commerce. Nonetheless, the government penalized Filburn for exceeding the Act's quotas. Filburn filed suit, arguing that the Act was unconstitutional. As he saw it, Congress had no right to regulate wheat that had no effect on interstate commerce.

The Supreme Court, however, held that the Commerce Clause gave Congress the power to regulate Filburn's personal store of wheat. The Court held that the Commerce Clause enabled Congress to regulate **intra**state activity that had a "substantial effect" on **inter**state commerce (sounds a lot like *Schechter Poultry*, right?).

In addition, the Court stated that Congress can regulate activity that has *no effect at all* on interstate commerce because when all such activity is added together, it has – as a group – a "substantial effect" on interstate commerce. Filburn's withholding of his personal wheat from the market, when added to all the rest of the wheat that was withheld from the market, had a "substantial effect" on interstate commerce. Therefore, Congress could regulate it under the Commerce Clause.

Key Takeaway from Wickard v. Filburn:
(1) *Wickard v. Filburn* was a massive expansion of Congress' power to regulate commerce. Congress could now regulate even activity that has no effect at all on interstate commerce because when all such activity is added together, it has – as a group – a "substantial effect" on interstate commerce.

18

Heart of Atlanta Motel v. United States (1964) & Katzenbach v. McClung (1964)

Congress enacted the Civil Rights Act of 1964 to protect the civil liberties of black Americans. The Act applied to any business whose operation affected interstate commerce. The Heart of Atlanta Motel refused to rent rooms to black Americans. It argued that the Civil Rights Act of 1964 was invalid because Congress exceeded its Commerce Clause power when it passed the Act. The Supreme Court held that Congress had not exceeded its power under the Commerce Clause when it passed the Civil Rights Act. This was because the motel was on a major highway and received 75% of its business from other states. Therefore, the motel's discrimination had an impact on interstate commerce and Congress could regulate it under the Commerce Clause.

Ollie McClung owned a barbecue restaurant on a major interstate in Birmingham, Alabama. He did not serve black Americans. Just like the motel, he argued that Congress lacked power under the Commerce Clause to enact the Civil Rights Act of 1964. The Supreme Court held that McClung was required to provide full restaurant access to black Americans. It stated that discrimination in restaurants had a significant impact on the interstate movement of food and products. Since this was commerce, Congress could regulate it. Therefore, the Civil Rights Act of 1964 was valid and McClung had to obey it.

Key Takeaways from Heart of Atlanta Motel v. United States & Katzenbach v. McClung:
(1) Racial discrimination impacts interstate commerce because it restricts interstate movement of those experiencing discrimination as well as interstate movement of materials and products. Therefore, Congress can regulate it under its Commerce Clause power.
(2) The Court held that it didn't matter that McClung didn't serve out-of-state customers because Congress' authority under the Commerce Clause extends to local activities that have a significant impact on interstate commerce. (Notice how similar this sounds to *Wickard v. Filburn*).

After the New Deal era, the expanded Commerce Clause was applied to a wide range of new and emerging issues, such as gun control and drug-use laws.

United States v. Lopez (1995) (*"the school guns case"*)

When Alfonzo Lopez was caught carrying a gun into his high school in San Antonio, Texas, he was charged with violating the Gun-Free School Zones Act of 1990. This Act prohibited the possession of firearms on school grounds. Lopez challenged the Act, arguing that it was unconstitutional because it exceeded Congress' power under the Commerce Clause.

The Supreme Court agreed with Lopez. In other words, Congress did not have power under the Commerce Clause to enact the Gun-Free School Zones Act. This was because the possession of a gun in a school zone is not a commercial activity that the federal government could regulate. It does not have a "substantial effect" on interstate commerce.

Key Takeaway from United States v. Lopez:
(1) The possession of a gun in a school zone does not have a "substantial effect" on interstate commerce.

Gonzales v. Raich (2005) (*"the marijuana case"*)

Congress enacted the Controlled Substances Act (CSA) in 1971. This Act banned the possession of marijuana. Soon afterward, the state of California passed the Compassionate Use Act, which legalized marijuana for medical uses.

Federal agents seized medically prescribed marijuana from a California resident's home. The homeowners sued the federal agents in court, arguing that Congress' power under the Commerce Clause did not authorize the passage of the CSA because marijuana use within the state of California was not part of interstate commerce. (Sounds a lot like the argument farmer Filburn tried to make in *Wickard*, right?).

The Supreme Court held that the Commerce Clause gave Congress the power to enact the CSA even though the marijuana usage only occurred in one state and was not economic in nature. This was because (here we go again) the use of marijuana in California had a "substantial effect" on interstate commerce.

—

20

<u>Key Takeaway from Gonzales v. Raich</u>:
(1) *Raich* was yet another expansion of Congress' power to regulate commerce. Before *Raich*, Congress could regulate intrastate **economic** activity (like selling crops in *Wickard*) that had a "substantial effect" on interstate commerce. After *Raich*, Congress could regulate intrastate **non-economic** activity (like using drugs) that had a "substantial effect" on interstate commerce.

National Federation of Independent Businesses v. Sebelius (2012) ("*the Obamacare case*")

Congress passed the Affordable Care Act (ACA) in 2010. The ACA included a mandate stating that anyone who didn't get health insurance by 2014 would have to pay a tax. The National Federation of Independent Businesses, along with 26 states, challenged the mandate, arguing that Congress did not have the power under the Commerce Clause to enact the mandate.

The Supreme Court held that the mandate was not a valid exercise of Congress' power to regulate commerce under the Commerce Clause. The mandate effectively forced people to participate in commerce. The Commerce Clause does not give Congress the power to regulate commercial **in**activity.

<u>Key Takeaway from National Federation of Independent Businesses v. Sebelius</u>:
(1) The Commerce Clause does not give Congress the power to regulate commercial **in**activity. It only applies to existing commercial activity.

SUMMING IT ALL UP
(1) The Commerce Clause gives Congress the ability to make laws that regulate interstate commerce (commerce between states).
(2) Congress can, under the Commerce Clause, regulate activities that have the mere *potential* to affect interstate commerce.
(3) The Commerce Clause also enables Congress to regulate **intra**state activity (activity occurring entirely within one state) that *substantially affects* **inter**state commerce (activity between states).

(2) Congress can regulate activity that has no effect at all on interstate commerce because when all such activity is added together, it has – as a group – a "substantial effect" on interstate commerce.

(3) The Commerce Clause does not give Congress the power to regulate economic **in**activity.

THINGS TO THINK ABOUT

(1) The Commerce Clause has clearly expanded over time. Is this a good thing? A bad thing? A little bit of both?

(2) Are *Wickard* and *Sebelius* contradictory? *Sebelius* states that Congress cannot regulate economic inactivity. But *Wickard* held that Congress could regulate crops grown for personal use under its Commerce Clause power. Aren't home-use crops the epitome of economic inactivity? Would allowing Congress to regulate the farmer's home-use crops essentially be allowing Congress to do exactly what *Sebelius* prohibits?

CHAPTER 5: THE LEGISLATIVE POWER – THE TAXING & SPENDING CLAUSE

Under the Taxing & Spending Clause, Congress has the power to collect taxes and spend money. The following two cases explain some of the limits on that power.

South Dakota v. Dole (1987) (*"the drinking age case"*)

In 1984, Congress enacted a law that withheld 5% of a state's highway funds if it didn't raise its minimum drinking age to 21. South Dakota's drinking age was 19. South Dakota argued that the law was unconstitutional because it exceeded Congress' power under the Taxing & Spending Clause.

The Supreme Court upheld the law. The law reasonably pursued the general welfare, so it was valid under the Taxing & Spending Clause.

Key Takeaway from South Dakota v. Dole:

(1) To be valid under the Taxing & Spending Clause, a law must reasonably pursue the general welfare.

National Federation of Independent Businesses v. Sebelius (2012) (*"the Obamacare case"*)

Remember this case from last chapter? Here's a quick refresher.

Congress passed the Affordable Care Act (ACA) in 2010. The ACA included a mandate stating that anyone who didn't get health insurance by 2014 would have to pay a tax. The National Federation of Independent Businesses challenged the mandate, arguing that Congress did not have the power under the Taxing & Spending Clause to enact the mandate.

The Supreme Court held that Congress *did* have the power under the Taxing & Spending Clause to mandate people to buy health insurance. The Court said that the mandate was considered a tax (not a penalty), and since Congress has the power to tax, the mandate was valid.

Key Takeaway from National Federation of Independent Businesses v. Sebelius:
(1) Congress has the power under the Taxing & Spending Clause to require people to buy health insurance.

SUMMING IT ALL UP
(1) To be valid under the Taxing & Spending Clause, a law must be in reasonable pursuit of the general welfare.
(2) Congress has the power under the Taxing & Spending Clause to require people to buy health insurance.

THINGS TO THINK ABOUT
(1) *Sebelius* is a strange case because the proponents of the ACA themselves (including the President) repeatedly said that the mandate was a penalty, *not* a tax. If that is true, did the Court overstep its constitutional role to interpret – not make – the law? Chief Justice John Roberts admitted that calling the mandate a "tax" was not the natural reading of the ACA.
(2) *Sebelius* is also a bizarre case in light of Chapter 4. The Court managed to say that under one if its powers (the power to regulate interstate commerce), Congress *could not* enact the mandate, but under another one of its powers (the power to tax), Congress *could* enact the mandate.

CHAPTER 6: THE LEGISLATIVE POWER – THE NECESSARY & PROPER CLAUSE

Article I contains a long list of Congressional powers, and the Necessary & Proper Clause comes at the end of that list. It gives Congress the ability to make laws that are necessary and proper for putting the Constitution into action.

McCulloch v. Maryland is a very famous case about the Necessary & Proper Clause:

McCulloch v. Maryland (1819) (*"the national bank case"*)

As the United States began to get its footing after the Revolutionary War, Congress established a national bank. The state of Maryland argued that Congress did not have the ability to create a national bank.

The Supreme Court held that Congress had the power to create a national bank under the Necessary & Proper Clause of Article I. Even though the Constitution did not expressly give Congress the power to create a national bank, Congress could do so because it was "necessary and proper" for Congress to carry out its listed responsibilities in Article I, which include things like collecting revenue and levying taxes.

Key Takeaways from McCulloch v. Maryland:
(1) Congress' power under the Necessary & Proper Clause of Article I includes the power to write laws that are "necessary and proper" for implementing the Constitution. It includes the ability to make laws that aren't necessarily specified in Congress' powers under the Constitution.
(2) In *McCulloch*, the Court held that creating a national bank was a "necessary and proper" use of Congress' power to carry out its listed responsibilities in Article I.

United States v. Comstock (2010)

The Adam Walsh Child Protection & Safety Act extended federal prison sentences for mentally ill sex offenders. Several convicted sex offenders filed suit, arguing that Congress did not have the power to enact this law.

The Supreme Court held that Congress *did* have the power to enact this law under the Necessary & Proper Clause, which allows Congress to make laws that are necessary and proper for carrying out its listed responsibilities in Article I. The Court held that this law was necessary to protect communities and children, which is *not* one of Congress' listed responsibilities in Article I.

Key Takeaways from United States v. Comstock:
(1) The Adam Walsh Child Protection & Safety Act was valid because it was necessary and proper for protecting communities and children.
(2) The Necessary & Proper Clause allows Congress to make any laws that are necessary and proper for carrying out its listed responsibilities in Article I. In *McCulloch*, the national bank was necessary and proper for carrying out Congress' listed responsibilities for collecting revenue and taxes. Protecting communities and children, however, is *not* one of Congress' listed responsibilities in Article I. Does this mean that the Adam Walsh Child Protection & Safety Act was actually invalid?

National Federal of Independent Businesses v. Sebelius (2012) ("*the Obamacare case*")

I know, this case starting to get old.

But *Sebelius* had a lot of angles, and the Necessary & Proper Clause was one of them. So here's one more quick review:

Congress passed the Affordable Care Act (ACA) in 2010. The ACA included a mandate stating that anyone who didn't get health insurance by 2014 would have to pay a tax. The National Federation of Independent Businesses challenged the mandate. As we saw in Chapter 5, the Supreme Court upheld the mandate as a valid use of Congress' Taxing & Spending power because the mandate was considered a tax.

The Necessary & Proper Clause also came into play. The question was: is it "proper" for Congress to require American citizens to buy health insurance? In other words, is it proper for Congress to force individual people to do business with private health insurance companies? The Court said no, it was not proper for Congress to do this.

Key Takeaway from National Federation of Independent Businesses v. Sebelius:
(1) It is not proper for Congress to force American citizens to do business with private health insurance companies.

SUMMING IT ALL UP
(1) Congress' power under the Necessary & Proper Clause of Article I is broad and powerful. It gives Congress the power to write laws that are "necessary and proper" for implementing Congress' listed powers in Article I.
(2) Congress' power under this provision even includes interfering with commerce within a single state, as long as it is deemed "necessary and proper" to do so to carry out Congress' power to regulate commerce.
(3) It is not "proper" for Congress to force American citizens to do business with private health insurance companies.

THINGS TO THINK ABOUT
(1) What is the limit of the Necessary & Proper Clause? How far can Congress go before something is not necessary or proper? And what about the *Comstock*-type situation where Congress is doing something that is not included in its list of Article I powers?

CHAPTER 7: THE JUDICIAL BRANCH

Article III of the Constitution is all about the judicial branch.

How much power does the judiciary have? Article III says that the judicial power extends to all cases and controversies "arising under this Constitution [and] the laws of the United States." That's sort-of helpful, but it still doesn't give us any guidelines on how a federal judge is supposed to decide cases. That's where *Marbury v. Madison* comes in.

Marbury v. Madison (1803) (*"the judges case"*)

The facts of *Marbury* are complicated, but the key thing you need to know is that it contains a very important statement about the role of the judge. Chief Justice John Marshall wrote: "It is emphatically the province and duty of the judicial department to say what the law is." **Judges are supposed to say what the law *is*, not what it *should be*.**

Key Takeaways from Marbury v. Madison:
(1) Judges cannot make laws or say what the law should be – that is not part of their job description. Their job is only to state what the law is and apply the law to the facts.

Three of the most important authors of the Constitution – James Madison, Alexander Hamilton, and John Jay – wrote a series of documents called The Federalist Papers around the time the Constitution was being drafted. They used The Federalist Papers to explain the Constitution to the public. In Federalist Paper #78, they wrote that the judiciary's job was to ensure the "impartial administration of the laws." They also said that the courts can never create laws. These statements line up with *Marbury*.

Federal judges have lifetime tenure. Does that mean they can do whatever they want without any consequences? Is lifetime tenure a good idea? In the end, it is. Think about it: if judges were elected, they would make political decisions for the people who elected them. And those decisions would not be neutral at all. They would be very biased. That would contradict the goal of having an impartial judiciary.

* * * * *

Those are the basics on the judicial branch. But there's one more thing you should know about: the toolbox judges use to make decisions. This is important because the Supreme Court cases that create so much interest every year are decided using the tools in this toolbox. If you understand these tools, you'll be able to understand why certain cases end up the way they do and why some judges think differently than others. And once you understand that, you'll

27

be able to argue persuasively in your own communities about why your position is the best one.

Picture a pair of sunglasses with yellow-tinted lenses. When you look through those lenses, the entire world is tinted yellow. If you put on a pair of sunglasses with green-tinted lenses, the whole world suddenly looks green. The same is true with how judges interpret the Constitution. There are different lenses through which judges view the law, and those lenses make all the difference. Switch the lens and the case looks entirely different. There are two primary lenses that judges use.

The first and most foundational lens is called **Originalism**. This lens believes that judges should make decisions based on the **original public meaning** of the document. In other words, what did the text mean to a member of the public at the time it was enacted? In order to figure this out, we look at the text of the law and the history of its formation. That meaning can then be applied to the case at hand. The meaning doesn't change – only the *application* of that meaning to new circumstances does. If you're interested in reading an Originalist opinion, check out Justice Clarence Thomas' opinion in *McDonald v. City of Chicago*. Justice Thomas bases his opinion on the text and history of the Second Amendment.

Why do originalists focus on the original public meaning? Professor Gary Lawson has a good explanation. Imagine that you find a very old fried chicken recipe from the 1700s. You'd like to try it out, but the recipe is so old you can hardly understand it. You're not even sure what some of those ingredients are. How do you go about determining what the fried chicken recipe really means?

You would seek to figure out what it meant to a person at the time it was written, of course. We all know the meaning of the recipe is fixed. No matter how much you want to, you can't turn it into a recipe for lentil soup. The recipe is also a public document, so its meaning is something that the average observer of that time would understand. If "add salt to taste" meant something different in the 1700s than it does today, you'd probably want to know that. Otherwise, you'd botch the entire recipe.

The same thing is true of determining what a law means. A law is written at a certain moment in time, and it is written for people living at that time and in that context. A law is a public thing, a thing that is meant to be understood by members of the public. In a lot of ways, a law is a recipe, addressed to the public, that is meant to be understood by the public. Therefore, when we want to understand a law's meaning, we want to understand what it meant to a member of the public at the time it was enacted. We want to figure out its original public meaning.

Being an Originalist requires paying a lot of attention to the text. Some people refer to this as Textualism, which is the idea that words mean what they conveyed to reasonable people at the time they were written.

Arguments For Originalism:
- This is just how language works. For instance, the word "deer" refers to a specific wild animal in today's language. But in 16th century English, "deer" referred to a wide range of animals. Disregarding the original public meaning in that instance would lead to a totally incorrect understanding of the text.
- Originalism remembers that law is a public thing, not a private thing that depends on secret intentions or hidden agendas.
- Originalism doesn't mandate a particular outcome – it simply grounds the judge's starting point in the most logical, common-sense, and observable source we have. The text and history are factual, tangible things. A judge's sense of "modern notions of decency," on the other hand, are not.
- Originalism is deeply democratic. The Constitution is validated by the "consent of the governed." (Remember Chapter 1?). Allowing Courts to change the meaning of the Constitution therefore overrides that consent and disregards the political participation of the American people.
- Originalism is inherent in the very idea of having a rule of law. Why write down the law if it can be bypassed by judges based on their personal preferences? For that matter, why bother having the law at all? Isn't the whole point of writing it down to ensure that it remains?
- Originalism is, in a way, the very reason we have judges. The point of the judicial branch is to apply and interpret the law in

cases and controversies arising under the laws of the United States. Originalism holds them to that task and ensures that the law is applied to all people using a single standard. Other approaches disregard this fair application in favor of the judge's personal views.

Arguments Against Originalism:
- Many claim that Originalism would keep us stuck in the past. This is called the "Dead Hand Objection." It argues that the Constitution was written a long time ago and doesn't line up with modern society. We shouldn't allow their "dead hands" to reach into the present age. (This is more of an objection to the idea of having a rule of law in the first place. After all, by this logic, aren't statutes passed last week "dead hands of the past"?).
- It's too hard. Originalism requires lots of historical research and it requires the judge to submit his opinions to those of the Constitution.
- Originalism doesn't give us a clear answer every time. It only gives us a starting point.
- Others simply argue that Originalism doesn't create results they like. It may be a subjective criticism, but it is worth noting.

The second lens is called **Living Constitutionalism**. This lens believes that the Constitution is a **living, evolving document** that should be updated over time based on society's changing beliefs. It is essentially the legal application of Darwin's theory of evolution. Living Constitutionalism doesn't look at the original public meaning of the law; it looks at the meaning that today's society would give the law. If you're interested in reading a Living Constitutionalist opinion, check out Justice Anthony Kennedy's opinion in *Obergefell v. Hodges*. Justice Kennedy bases the decision on modern philosophical notions of autonomy and decency.

Arguments For Living Constitutionalism:
- Living Constitutionalism focuses on trying to keep the law up to date with modern society's notions of what is good, fair, and right.
- The legislative process is difficult. It takes forever. Living Constitutionalism bypasses the long, laborious legislative process and gets us to a result more easily.

- Living Constitutionalism creates results that modern people are more likely to approve of.
- Judges are some of the most intelligent people in society. They are, in a way, the "wise elders" of our culture. Any large decisions should be left to them, not regular citizens.

Arguments Against Living Constitutionalism:
- Living Constitutionalism is subjective. It is based on the judge's personal preferences. Almost all the cases we look back on with disgust (*Dred Scott v. Sandford*, for instance – see Chapter 25) are a result of judges who disregarded Originalism for Living Constitutionalism.
- Living Constitutionalism contradicts the idea of the rule of law in the first place. Why write down the law – in fact, why have it all – if it can be overruled any time a judge feels like it?
- The Constitution includes a provision (Article V) that lays out how it can be changed. That change process ensures that change only occurs when it is widely accepted by the American people. Living Constitutionalism, on the other hand, bypasses the American people by giving judges the ability to make changes by themselves.
- Living Constitutionalism isn't fair. Whereas Originalism is based on things everyone can see – the text and history – Living Constitutionalism is based on whatever is inside a particular judge's head. Everyone who comes before that judge is therefore subject to his personal whims, which doesn't seem very fair.

SUMMING IT ALL UP
(1) The judicial power extends to all cases and controversies "arising under this Constitution [and] the laws of the United States."
(2) Judges cannot make laws or write policy – that is not part of their job description. Their job is only to state what the law is and apply that law to the facts.
(3) One way of viewing the Constitution is called **Originalism**. This view believes that we should look at the text and history in order to understand the **original public meaning** of the document. In other words, what did the text mean to a member of the public at the time it was enacted? Another way of viewing the Constitution is called **Living Constitutionalism**. This view believes that the Constitution is a **living, evolving document** that

should be updated over time based on society's changing beliefs. Every controversial Supreme Court case can eventually be boiled down to the conflict between these two lenses. Keep an eye out for them in the future!

CHAPTER 8: THE EXECUTIVE BRANCH

We've covered the first and second branches of the American government. It's time to tackle the third and final branch: the Executive (i.e., the President).

The Executive branch is established in Article II of the Constitution. The Executive must "take care that the laws be faithfully executed." The President is responsible for making sure that the law is enforced. Other than that, the President only has a few powers:

- Acting as the Commander in Chief of the Army & Navy
- Granting pardons
- Making treaties
- Nominating federal judges, ambassadors, and agency officials
- Giving an annual State of the Union message
- The Veto power
- Filling Senate vacancies that open up when the Senate is not in session.

People are often surprised to learn how little power the President has. Americans today tend to view the President as a king-like figure who has unlimited power. But the framers wanted Congress to make the big decisions, not the President. Having an all-powerful "king" would have put them right back in the European monarchies they and their ancestors had left.

The following cases show how we've come to understand the limits of the Executive power. Many of them also provide a great review on the separation of powers.

Youngstown Sheet & Tube Company v. Sawyer (1952) (*"the steel mills case"*)

During the Korean War, President Harry Truman issued an executive order directing the Secretary of Commerce to seize control over every steel mill in the United States. The purpose of this executive order was to head off a potential strike by the United Steelworkers of America. Did President Truman have the authority to do this?

The Supreme Court held that he did not. The executive order was invalid.

Remember our discussion of the separation of powers in Chapter 2? Power is separated into three branches, each of which have separate responsibilities. *Youngstown* reinforces this system of separated powers because it concludes that the President can only act within the sphere of the Executive power. He can't step outside that sphere and start making laws – that's Congress' job.

In other words: stay in your lane, President Truman.

Key Takeaways from Youngstown Sheet & Tube Company v. Sawyer:
(1) The President's power must stem from the Constitution itself or an Act of Congress.
(2) In our separated-powers government, the President does not make the laws. Allowing the President to act where there is no Constitutional or statutory authority would be the equivalent of allowing him to make laws.

Korematsu v. United States (1944)

After the bombing of Pearl Harbor in December 1941, President Franklin D. Roosevelt issued Executive Order 9066, which required all Japanese Americans to move into relocation camps. This was done during a time of widespread fear of Japanese military aggression. Fred Korematsu, a Japanese man, refused to go to the relocation camp. He argued that the President did not have the authority to restrict the rights of Japanese Americans in this manner.

The Supreme Court upheld both Korematsu's conviction and the President's creation of relocation camps for Japanese Americans. The Court said that the Executive Order was valid because it was done in the interest of preventing sabotage by Japanese spies. The wartime context meant that the President had additional authority.

Korematsu has since been overruled. It has become clear that this decision was a clear violation of the constitutional rights of Japanese Americans.

Key Takeaway from Korematsu v. United States:
(1) The Executive has additional powers during wartime, but this power is not a license to violate constitutional rights.

Nixon v. Fitzgerald (1982)

Fitzgerald sued U.S. President Richard Nixon for illegally firing him. Nixon asserted that he was immune from this lawsuit because Presidents are not liable for actions taken while in office. The question for the Supreme Court was: is the President immune from lawsuits regarding his official acts as President?

The Supreme Court answered that he was. In other words, Fitzgerald could *not* sue President Nixon for what Nixon had done while serving as President.

Key Takeaway from Nixon v. Fitzgerald:
(1) The U.S. President has immunity for official actions taken while serving as President.

Morrison v. Olson (1988)

An Independent Counsel named Morrison was appointed under the Ethics in Government Act of 1978 to investigate an executive branch official named Olson. Morrison served Olson with a subpoena. Olson refused to respond to the subpoena, arguing that the power given to the Independent Counsel unconstitutionally intruded on the Executive Power.

The Supreme Court held that the power given to the Independent Counsel did **not** unconstitutionally intrude on the Executive Power. This was because even though the Independent Counsel was doing things that were inherently part of the Executive branch's function, the intrusion on Executive Power was minimal.

Key Takeaways from Morrison v. Olson:
(1) An Independent Counsel's power to investigate an Executive branch official – an activity that is inherently part of the

Executive power – did **not** unconstitutionally intrude on the Executive Power because the intrusion was minimal.

Clinton v. New York (1998) (*"the veto case"*)

Under the Line Item Veto Act, the President could cancel portions of spending bills that he did not agree with. President Bill Clinton canceled a provision of the Balanced Budget Act of 1997. He later canceled part of the Taxpayer Relief Act of 1997. Both cancellations were challenged in court. The challengers argued that the ability to select and cancel portions of bills exceeded the scope of the Executive Power and therefore violated the separation of powers.

The Supreme Court agreed with the challengers. In other words, the Executive could *not* selectively cancel portions of bills because that enabled him to exercise the law-making power that was reserved for the Legislative Branch (Congress).

Key Takeaway from Clinton v. New York:
(1) The Line Item Veto Act, which allowed the President to cancel certain portions of bills, was unconstitutional because it allowed the President to overstep the boundaries of the Executive Power. This violated the separation of powers.

Seila Law, LLC v. Consumer Financial Protection Bureau (2020)

The Consumer Financial Protection Bureau (CFPB) – a federal executive agency – opened an investigation into a law firm called Seila Law, LLC. It demanded that Seila Law turn over a large number of documents. Seila refused to do so. A federal district court ordered Seila to provide the requested documents. Seila appealed, arguing that the CFPB's structure violated the separation of powers because it was led by an independent agency director who uses Executive power but can only be removed by the President for good cause. In other words, Seila argued that the fact that the President could not remove the CFPB's independent agency director whenever he wanted was a violation of the separation of powers.

The Supreme Court agreed. It held that the CFPB was unconstitutionally structured. The President needed to have the authority to remove the CFPB head any time – and for any reason. This because Article II gives the Executive power to the President alone; it doesn't split the Executive power between the President and agency directors.

Key Takeaway from Seila Law LLC v. Consumer Financial Protection Bureau:
(1) Anyone who uses Executive power must be under the complete control of the Executive.

SUMMING IT ALL UP

(1) The Executive branch (the President) is responsible for enforcing (not making) the law.
(2) Overall, the Executive's responsibilities are quite limited.
(3) The President has immunity for official actions taken while serving as President.
(4) In our separated-powers government, the President does not make laws. His power must stem from the Constitution or an Act of Congress. Allowing the President to act where there is no Constitutional authority would be the equivalent of allowing him to make laws.
(5) Anyone who uses Executive power must be under the complete control of the Executive.

THINGS TO THINK ABOUT

(1) The Executive power is expanding. There are many examples of this. Take, for instance, the increase in the number of Executive Orders (Presidential directives regarding legal changes he wants to see). These bring the President ever closer to making the law, which isn't in his job description. Another example is the expansion of the Executive's power through presidentially-appointed administrative agencies (see Chapter 30).
(2) Justice Antonin Scalia wrote a very famous dissenting opinion in *Morrison v. Olson*. He argued that the President should have *exclusive* control over the Executive branch. Notice how this lines up with the holding *Seila Law* that anyone who uses Executive power must be under the complete control of the Executive. What do you think of Justice Scalia's argument?

CHAPTER 9:
PRIVILEGES AND IMMUNITIES

Article IV has four sections. We are going to examine three of them.

SECTION 1

Section 1 is called the Full Faith & Credit Clause. It states that "full faith and credit shall be given in each state to the public acts, records, and judicial proceedings of every other state." In other words, Nebraska must honor the laws of Tennessee, and vice versa.

SECTION 2

Section 2 is very important. It is called the Privileges and Immunities Clause, and it protects the privileges and immunities of citizenship. This means that Idaho must treat citizens of Maine the same way that it would treat Idaho citizens. A great example is a 1984 Camden, New Jersey rule that required 40% of the city's workers to be Camden residents. This rule was held to be a violation of the Privileges and Immunities Clause because it discriminated against out-of-state workers regarding fundamental rights like the right to work.

What exactly *are* the "privileges and immunities" of United States citizenship? Well…we're not really sure. The Supreme Court has talked about the right to work, travel, own property, and other things as being "privileges and immunities." Overall, though, the "privileges and immunities" of American citizenship are still being debated.

Professor Randy Barnett of Georgetown Law School has done a lot of research on this topic. He believes that "privileges and immunities" includes:
(1) Fundamental rights that belong to the citizens of all free governments, such as the right to life, liberty, and the pursuit of happiness.
(2) The right to make and enforce contracts, the right to sue and give evidence, and the right to inherit, own, lease, sell, and buy property.

(3) The personal rights in the first eight amendments to the Constitution (i.e., the Bill of Rights) – the right to free exercise of religion, the right to speak and publish freely, the right to bear arms, the right to counsel, etc.

U.S. Supreme Court Justice Clarence Thomas has also examined the meaning of "privileges and immunities," and his conclusion is very similar to Barnett's. He concluded in *McDonald v. City of Chicago* that "privileges and immunities" includes at least the rights contained in the first 8 amendments to the Constitution (the Bill of Rights).

SECTION 4

Section 4 is called the Guarantee Clause. It states that the federal government will guarantee to every state "a republican form of government." This isn't talking about the Republican party of today. It is talking about a republican structure of government – people acting through their elected representatives (as opposed to a single monarch or no representatives at all). Each state is guaranteed a government that operates by the people acting through their elected representatives: the "consent of the governed" (Chapter 1). That is the hallmark of the American governmental system.

CHAPTER 10: HOW TO AMEND THE CONSTITUTION

If you want to amend the Constitution, look at Article V.

There are two ways to call a convention for amending the Constitution. The first way is by voting. This requires 2/3 of **both** houses – the Senate *and* the House of Representatives – to vote in favor of holding an amendment convention.

The second way is through the state legislatures. This requires 2/3 of the state legislatures to apply for an amendment convention. An amendment will be added to the Constitution if it is ratified by the legislatures of ¾ of the states. An amendment can be blocked by any thirteen states who decide to withhold their approval.

THINGS TO THINK ABOUT

(1) The amendment process hasn't been used in a long time. Why do you think that is?

CHAPTER 11: INTRODUCTION TO THE AMENDMENTS

Congratulations!

You've made it through the articles of the Constitution.

We are now going to get into the topics that you've probably heard more about – religion, free speech, police searches, Miranda rights, gun rights, abortion, and much more. The rest of the book is dedicated to the amendments to the Constitution. The first eight amendments are called the Bill of Rights. We'll start there.

Why do we have amendments? Before all the states had ratified the Constitution, many American leaders began to worry that the Constitution did not do enough to protect individual rights. Some of them wanted to add a Bill of Rights to the Constitution. Others opposed adding a Bill of Rights because they felt that it would provide the federal government with an almost unlimited way to expand its power. In the end, James Madison agreed to add a Bill of Rights to the Constitution. He did so in order to make sure that all the states signed on to the Constitution. If he hadn't, there may not have been a union at all.

One more thing before we get started. You may remember our discussion of a concept called "incorporation" way back in Chapter 2. Incorporation is the process of applying the Bill of Rights to the states (remember, the Bill of Rights originally applied only to the federal government). Over time, the Supreme Court has applied most of the Bill of Rights to the states. It has done so by using the Due Process Clause of the Fourteenth Amendment. The Court has reasoned that the protections of the Bill of Rights were *part of* the Fourteenth Amendment's guarantee of due process, and since the Fourteenth Amendment applied to the states, it could be used to apply the Bill of Rights to the states. Therefore, whenever the Court determines that a particular right is "fundamental to ordered liberty" or "deeply rooted in this Nation's history and tradition," it has used the Fourteenth Amendment to apply that right to the states. The result of this process has been that nearly all the amendments in the Bill of Rights have been applied to the states.

CHAPTER
12: ESTABLISHMENT OF RELIGION

You've probably heard television pundits or radio commentators talking about "free speech" or "religious liberty" at some point. Those topics – religion and speech – are what the First Amendment is all about.

There are three parts to the First Amendment. One deals with the free exercise of religion (the Free Exercise Clause), one deals with free speech (the Free Speech Clause), and one deals with the establishment of religion (the Establishment Clause). We'll start with the Establishment Clause.

The Establishment Clause says that the federal government cannot establish a national religion. By "establish," the framers were referring to federal government-enforced religious exercise. This was important to the framers because they and their ancestors had come from European contexts in which religion was often controlled or even mandated by the government. History had shown them that government-established religion only led to trouble.

Notice what the Establishment Clause doesn't do. It doesn't prohibit states from establishing or accommodating religion. It merely protects the states from any attempt by the federal government to establish a religion. In this sense, the Establishment Clause is all about federalism (the separation of power between the federal government and the states - see Chapter 2). It is designed to prevent Congress from interfering with state efforts to accommodate religion. The point of the Establishment Clause is to protect *religion* from *government*, not vice versa.

Given this background, it would seem impossible to apply the Establishment Clause to apply to the states (see Chapter 11 for a review of incorporation). If the whole point of the Establishment Clause is to prevent the federal government from messing with the states, how could it then be applied to the states? That would essentially bar them from doing the very thing the Establishment Clause is supposed to enable them to do. Yet the Establishment Clause *has* been applied to the states since 1947!

One more thing before we get to the cases. You may have heard the phrase "wall of separation between church and state." This phrase has come to define how we think about the Establishment Clause: as a wall between the church and the state. It comes from a letter Thomas Jefferson wrote to the Danbury Baptist Association in 1802, and it reflects Jefferson's personal view of the Establishment Clause. As it turns out, he was the *only one* who thought this way. No other framer saw the Establishment Clause as a "wall of separation between church and state." They all viewed the Establishment Clause as what it truly is: a prohibition on the establishment of a national religion. Unfortunately, even though it is both incorrect and unrepresentative, the "wall of separation" concept has been absorbed into the Establishment Clause. It has since been used to support many unfortunate developments in American society, including widespread discrimination against Catholics during the late 19th and early 20th centuries.

Here are some cases that reveal the contentious debates this country has had over the Establishment Clause:

Lemon v. Kurtzman (1971)

Pennsylvania and Rhode Island had statutes requiring the state to pay for aspects of non-public, non-secular religion. A group of citizens sued, arguing that these statutes violated the Establishment Clause by requiring the government to pay for religious education.

The Supreme Court held that these statutes violated the Establishment Clause because they entangled the government with religion. The Court also developed a 3-part test for determining whether there has been a violation of the Establishment Clause.

(1) The statute must have a secular purpose.

(2) The statute's primary effect must not be to promote or inhibit religion.

(3) The statute must not foster excessive government entanglement with religion.

If that sounds like legalese to you, you're not alone. Since this case was decided, almost everyone (including the Supreme Court) has decided that the *Lemon* test is confusing, self-contradictory, and unworkable.

Key Takeaway from Lemon v. Kurtzman:
(1) There is a 3-part *Lemon* test for determining whether there has been a violation of the Establishment Clause. It is widely disfavored.

Lynch v. Donnelly (1983)

The city of Pawtucket, Rhode Island had put up an annual Christmas display in the shopping district for over 40 years. This display included a Santa Clause house, a banner stating "Season's Greetings," and a nativity scene. Daniel Donnelly sued Pawtucket mayor Dennis Lynch, claiming that the nativity scene violated the Establishment Clause.

The Supreme Court held that the city had not violated the Establishment Clause because the display was not an attempt to share a religious message. It was just a mixed Christmas season display. The secular items surrounding the display tempered the religious nature of the display.

Lynch also gave us a much simpler alternative to the *Lemon* test. It asks whether the purpose of the action is to endorse religion. If so, there is a violation of the Establishment Clause.

Key Takeaways from Lynch v. Donnelly:
(1) A longstanding mixed Christmas display that doesn't try to share a religious message does not violate the Establishment Clause.
(2) Endorsement Test: is the purpose of the action to endorse religion? If so, there is a violation of the Establishment Clause.

County of Allegheny v. ACLU (1989) (*"the reindeer case"*)

The Allegheny County courthouse had a small Christmas display on its front lawn that included a creche (a model depiction of Jesus' birth). The Pittsburgh City Council had a small Christmas display on its front law that included a menorah (a lamp representing Chanukah). The American Civil Liberties Union (ACLU) claimed that these displays violated the Establishment Clause.

The Supreme Court held that the menorah did not violate the Establishment Clause but the creche did. This was because the creche was explicitly religious, but the menorah was both religious and secular. The difference turned on the context, or the items surrounding the displays. For instance, the Court noted that there were no secular items (such as plastic reindeer) around the creche to temper its religious nature, but the menorah was surrounded by secular items that minimized its perceived religious message.

Key Takeaway from County of Allegheny v. ACLU:
(1) A public display of a creche violated the Establishment Clause, but a public display of a menorah did not. This was because, according to the Court, there were not enough secular objects alongside the creche to temper its religious nature.

In recent years, there has been an increase in cases involving religious schools. These cases are usually based on the claim that allowing a religious school to participate in a state funding program (like a scholarship program) would result in state money going to a religious school, thereby violating the Establishment Clause. Here's what the Supreme Court has said about that argument:

Zelman v. Simmons-Harris (2002) (*"the voucher case"*)

The state of Ohio established a scholarship program that gave Cleveland-area students financial aid vouchers to attend private schools. The vast majority of the private schools in that area happened to be religious. A group of taxpayers claimed the program violated the Establishment Clause because it indirectly gave government money to religious schools.

The Supreme Court held that the program did not violate the Establishment Clause. The fact that the majority of the schools in that area happened to be religious did not necessarily mean there was an Establishment Clause violation. This was a neutral program that offered parents the choice of where to send their children. Whether funds reached religious entities was entirely a parental choice – the government had nothing to do with it.

Key Takeaways from Zelman v. Simmons-Harris:
(1) A scholarship program that offers parents the choice of where to send their children does not violate the Establishment Clause, even if some of the participating schools are religious.
(2) The fact that a majority of schools in an area happen to be religious doesn't mean that there has been an Establishment of Religion.

McCreary County v. ACLU of Kentucky (2005) & Van Orden v. Perry (2005)

The hallway of the McCreary County, Kentucky courthouse contained a large display of the Ten Commandments. The American Civil Liberties Union (ACLU) argued that the display violated the Establishment Clause. The Supreme Court agreed. The display violated the Establishment Clause because its purpose was to endorse religion.

The Texas State Capitol grounds contained a 6-foot-high stone monument of the Ten Commandments. A homeless, disbarred lawyer named Thomas Van Orden argued that having this monument on the state capitol grounds was an establishment of religion. The Supreme Court disagreed with him. The monument did not violate the Establishment Clause because it communicated both a religious *and* secular message and was not intended to endorse religion.

<u>Key Takeaway from McCreary County v. ACLU of Kentucky & Van Orden v. Perry</u>:
(1) Having religious content or promoting a message consistent with religious doctrine doesn't automatically violate the Establishment Clause. What matters more is whether the point of the monument is to endorse religion.

Town of Greece v. Galloway (2014) (*"the town prayer case"*)

Board meetings in the town of Greece, New York began with a prayer given by a member of the local clergy. There was no policy excluding any particular faiths from giving this prayer, nor was there any evidence of discrimination against any religions. However, because the dominant religion in that area was Christianity, most of the prayers ended up being given by Christian ministers. Susan Galloway sued the town, arguing that the prayer practice violated the Establishment Clause by preferring Christianity over other faiths.

The Supreme Court held that the Town of Greece's policy did not violate the Establishment Clause. This was a historic and non-discriminatory prayer practice. Just because Christianity is the dominant religion in that area doesn't mean that the government is trying to establish Christianity as the official religion (sounds a little bit like *Zelman*, doesn't it?).

<u>Key Takeaways from Town of Greece v. Galloway</u>:
(1) Religious legislative prayer is allowed under the Establishment Clause.
(2) Just because one religion is more common in a particular region than another doesn't mean that the government is trying to establish that religion.

American Legion v. American Humanist Association (2019) (*"the cross case"*)

A public park in Bladensburg, Maryland includes a 40-foot-tall cross, built in 1918 to honor the veterans of World War I. Several Maryland residents claimed that they were offended by the cross because it seemed like a governmental endorsement of religion. They sued the public commission that maintained the cross, alleging a violation of the Establishment Clause.

The Supreme Court held that the cross did not violate the Establishment Clause. While the cross may have originated as a religious symbol, this particular cross has a secular meaning: memorializing WWI veterans. It has historical importance beyond its religious connotation.

Key Takeaways from American Legion v. American Humanist Association:
(1) Merely being offended by a religiously affiliated symbol doesn't mean that you have an Establishment Clause claim.

SUMMING IT ALL UP

(1) The Establishment Clause says that the federal government cannot establish a national religion. As originally understood, it does not prohibit states from establishing or accommodating religion. It merely prevents the federal government from interfering with state efforts to accommodate religion.
(2) The Establishment Clause does not create a "wall of separation" between church and state. This was Thomas Jefferson's personal view; none of the other framers viewed the Establishment Clause this way. The original public meaning of the Establishment Clause has nothing to do with creating a "wall of separation."
(3) We have no idea how to determine whether there has been an Establishment Clause violation. At first, we thought the *Lemon* test would work. That was an epic fail. Then we tried the Endorsement test, but that may have been ruined by *Allegheny County*. Now we're trying a historical approach (*Galloway* & *American Legion*).
(4) A longstanding mixed Christmas display that doesn't try to share a religious message does not violate the Establishment Clause.
(5) A scholarship program that offers parents the choice of where to send their children does not violate the Establishment Clause, even if some of the participating schools are religious in nature.
(6) Being offended isn't enough. Just because you may find a particular symbol or practice offensive doesn't mean that there has been an Establishment Clause violation.

THINGS TO THINK ABOUT

(1) These cases reflect the steady growth of secularism and the decline of religion in America. Cases like *Lynch* or *Galloway* or *American Legion* didn't occur during the first half (or maybe even first three-quarters) of the American republic, but they are now quite common.

(2) Why do you think the "wall of separation" idea has caught on so strongly despite being incorrect and unrepresentative of the framers?

(3) Does the decision in *County of Allegheny* mean that a religious display is only acceptable if it is surrounded by non-religious items? If so, how much non-religious stuff is required? Do we need to make sure we place 2 plastic reindeer next to the creche, or 5? And based on what?

(4) Did this case ruin the Endorsement Test? Both displays had religious aspects, so both could have been taken as endorsements of religion. By the same standard, they were not evangelism tools, so both were *not* endorsements of religion. Either way, it would seem that they had to stand or fall together. Was the Court just picking and choosing which religious symbol it liked best? Is ok for the Court to prefer one religion over another?

CHAPTER 13: FREE EXERCISE OF RELIGION

The Free Exercise Clause is one of the most well-known parts of the Constitution. It says that the government cannot prohibit the free exercise of religion. Remember from our discussion of the Declaration of Independence that the framers saw rights like religious exercise as natural rights that existed prior to government. Therefore, the government does not *give* us the right to exercise our religion. We already have it. The government's only job is to *protect* the right to exercise our religion.

Why did the framers protect religious activity? Because they and their ancestors had seen that religion – and society as a whole – suffered under governments that limited the free exercise of religion. Therefore, they wanted to protect religious exercise so that it would thrive.

Why is it important for religious exercise to be free to thrive? For that matter, why should we protect religious exercise at all? After all, religious people often have views that are disagreeable to the rest of society. The answer is that **religion cultivates the kind of virtue that is necessary for the success of our republic**. Virtuous people are people who have the character to govern themselves, and people who can govern themselves are people who can successfully govern a republic.

How does religion cultivate virtue? It cultivates virtue by placing at the center of life a Sovereign that takes precedence over politics. A culture in which such Sovereigns can safely flourish is a culture that is inherently oriented toward transcendent, eternal truths rather than temporal, political arguments. Religion therefore turns the citizen away from the temptation of utopian dreams and toward the humility of political cooperation.

Don't get me wrong – there are other ways to cultivate virtue. But religion is by far the most widespread and effective way to create virtue in both the individual and society at large. In addition, it helps create a cohesive society by bringing people from all walks of life together under shared ideals. The framers recognized this very positive aspect of religion and wanted to give it strong constitutional protections. But don't just take my word for it:

Ben Franklin: "Only a virtuous people are capable of freedom."

John Adams: "The only foundation of a free Constitution is pure virtue."

Again, John Adams: "Our Constitution was made only for a moral and religious people."

George Washington: "Whatever may be conceded to the influence of refined education on minds of peculiar structure, reason and experience both forbid us to expect that national morality can prevail in exclusion of religious principles."

George Washington again: "Let us with caution indulge the supposition that morality can be maintained without religion."

George Washington yet again: "Of all the dispositions and habits which lead to political prosperity, religion and morality are indispensable supports."

Gouverneur Morris: "[R]eligion is the only solid base of morals[,] and . . . morals are the only possible support of free governments."

Even Thomas Jefferson, who was at most a nominal Deist, stated that the liberties of this nation would become insecure if they were removed from their religious basis.

Foreign observers also saw that religion was necessary if America was to succeed. French thinker Alexander de Tocqueville was struck by the religious nature of the people during his visit to the United States in 1835. He said that "religion is more needed in democratic republics than in any others" because it discourages citizens from harming the republic through rash or imprudent actions.

In sum, the framers saw that religion cultivates the kind of virtue that is necessary for the success of our republic. Virtuous people are people who have the character to govern themselves, and people who can govern themselves are people who can successfully govern a republic. And religion was the best way to create this kind of large-scale virtue in a country as diverse as the United States.

* * * * *

Before we get started with this chapter, there is one concept that you'll need to understand: Levels of Scrutiny.

Imagine you're a track and field athlete. You like all the events, but your specialty is the high jump. Let's say you're interested in qualifying for your local track and field tournament. In order to do so, you'll have to jump over a bar set at 5 feet high. Now let's say you're interested in qualifying for the Olympics. This is a much more serious interest (or, one might say, a much higher bar). In order to qualify for the Olympics, you must jump over a bar set at 8 feet high. That's no joke.

The same thing is true for how courts decide whether a law is valid or not. They can apply a low bar (called Rational Basis Scrutiny) or a high bar (called Strict Scrutiny). **Rational Basis Scrutiny** requires only that the law be **rationally related to a legitimate government interest**. In other words, there only needs to be a good-enough government interest, and the law only needs to be somewhat related to it. **Strict Scrutiny**, on the other hand, requires that the law be **narrowly tailored to a compelling government interest**. The government must have a very strong interest, and the law must be very specifically tailored to meet that interest. It all depends on the kind of interest that is at stake.

As you can see, Strict Scrutiny is much harder to satisfy than Rational Basis. Therefore, if the court uses Strict Scrutiny to evaluate whether a law is valid or not, the law is *less* likely to be valid. This is because it will have to meet a high standard (high bar). On the other hand, if the court uses Rational Basis Scrutiny to evaluate whether a law is valid or not, the law is *more* likely to be valid. This is because it only has to meet a low standard (low bar).

Until 1990, all laws that dealt with the free exercise of religion received Strict Scrutiny. Americans were suspicious of restrictions on religious exercise and wanted to apply a high bar to any laws that tried to do so. The government therefore had to have a very strong interest before it could interfere with the free exercise of religion. This all changed in 1990 with the case of *Employment Division v. Smith*.

Employment Division v. Smith (1990) (*"the peyote case"*)

Two drug rehabilitation counselors in Oregon used a drug called peyote as part of a Native American religious ritual. They were fired from their jobs under an Oregon law that prohibited the use of peyote. They filed an unemployment benefits claim with the Employment Division but were denied. The two counselors sued, arguing that they were fired from their jobs for exercising their religion. Did the Oregon law prohibiting peyote use violate the Free Exercise Clause?

The Supreme Court held that the Oregon state law did *not* violate the Free Exercise Clause. In other words, the two counselors lost; the rehabilitation center was correct to fire them. "The Court has never held that an individual's religious beliefs excuse him from compliance with an otherwise valid law prohibiting conduct that the government is free to regulate." In other words, **the government has NO duty to provide a religious exemption from a generally applicable law**, even if not giving the exemption substantially burdens religion.

Key Takeaway from Employment Division v. Smith:
(1) The government does not have to provide a religious exemption from a generally applicable law. As long as the law applies to everyone, the government does not have to provide any exemptions for religious Americans – even if compliance with the law would force them to violate their religious beliefs.

Smith shocked everyone because it essentially opened the door for governments to make laws that infringed on religious beliefs with no fear of consequences. *Smith* left us with lots of big questions, like: when *does* the government have a duty to provide a religious exemption?

The following case is an example of when the government must provide a religious exemption from a generally applicable law under the *Smith* standard.

Church of Lukumi Babalu Aye, Inc. v. City of Hialeah (1993) (*"the animal sacrifice case"*)

51

A Santeria church in Hialeah, Florida included animal sacrifice as a form of worship. The city council was disturbed by this practice, so it passed 3 ordinances that prohibited the possession of animals for sacrifice without a state license. The church sued, arguing that these ordinances violated the Free Exercise Clause by singling out their religious exercise for negative treatment.

The Supreme Court held that these ordinances violated the Free Exercise Clause. Remember: under *Smith*, if a law applies to everyone, the government has no duty to provide religious exemptions. But the Court saw that the law in *Lukumi* did not apply to everyone. In fact, it was targeted directly at the church! Therefore, the government *did* have a duty to provide a religious exemption from the law.

Key Takeaway from Church of Lukumi Babalu Aye, Inc. v. City of Hialeah:
(1) If the law is *not* generally applicable, the government *does* have a duty to provide a religious exemption from it. Directly targeting a religious entity or practice is a sign that the law is *not* generally applicable.

Smith caused such an outrage that Congress immediately passed the Religious Freedom Restoration Act (RFRA), which restored the religious freedom protections *Smith* had destroyed. In particular, it restored the Strict Scrutiny standard for Free Exercise Clause issues. Although RFRA only applies to the federal government (not the states), many states also have their own RFRA statutes now.

Burwell v. Hobby Lobby Stores (2014)

The Green family owns Hobby Lobby, a nationwide arts and crafts store that employs over 13,000 people. As Christians, the Greens believe that contraception and abortion are wrong. However, the Affordable Care Act (ACA, also known as Obamacare) required all employers to provide contraception to their employees. The Greens challenged this requirement as a violation of the Free Exercise Clause and RFRA.

The Supreme Court ruled in favor of Hobby Lobby. The ACA forced religious corporations to violate their faith, and that was exactly the kind of thing that RFRA was meant to prevent.

A big question in this case was whether Hobby Lobby's status as a for-profit organization made a difference. Are for-profit companies "persons"? Yes, they are. The Court stated that they were considered legal "persons" whose religious liberty can be violated.

Key Takeaways from Burwell v. Hobby Lobby Stores:
(1) The ACA's contraception mandate violated the Religious Freedom Restoration Act and the Free Exercise Clause of the First Amendment by forcing religious people and corporations to violate their faith.
(2) For-profit corporations are legal "persons" whose religious liberty can be violated. They are protected by RFRA.

Trinity Lutheran Church of Columbia v. Comer (2017) ("*the playground case*")

Trinity Lutheran Church of Columbia, Missouri operates a preschool and daycare as part of its ministry. These ministries include daily religious instruction and prayer.

The Missouri Department of Natural Resources (DNR) offered a Playground Scrap Tire Surface Material Grant to any organizations who wanted to use recycled tires to resurface playgrounds. Trinity Lutheran applied for one of these grants but was denied. The DNR reasoned that giving a grant to Trinity Lutheran would essentially be funding the church with government money, which would violate the Establishment Clause. Trinity Lutheran sued, arguing that it had been excluded solely because of its religion in violation of the Free Exercise Clause.

The Supreme Court held that Trinity Lutheran was right. The DNR discriminated against Trinity Lutheran because of its religion. This kind of discrimination violates the Free Exercise Clause.

Key Takeaway from Trinity Lutheran Church of Columbia v. Comer:
(1) The exclusion of churches from a neutral funding program violated the Free Exercise Clause because it discriminated on the basis of religion.

Espinoza v. Montana Department of Revenue (2020)

A Montana scholarship program provided scholarships for children to attend private schools. Shortly after the program's creation, the Montana Department of Revenue issued Rule 1, which prohibited scholarship recipients from using scholarship funds to attend religious schools. The Department said that Rule 1 was necessary to comply with Article X, Section 6 of the Montana Constitution, which prohibits public aid to churches and religious schools. Since over 70% of Montana's private schools are religiously affiliated, Rule 1 threatened to undermine the entire scholarship program. Kendra Espinoza, who was unable to send her children to private religious school because of Rule 1, challenged it in court. The question for the U.S. Supreme Court was: can state governments bar religious organizations from participation in a generally available student aid program purely because the program affords students the choice of attending religious schools?

The Supreme Court held that they cannot. "A state . . . cannot disqualify some private schools solely because they are religious." Notice how both *Trinity Lutheran* and *Espinoza* establish the same concept: states can't exclude religious entities from public programs on the basis of their religion.

Key Takeaways from Espinoza v. Montana Department of Revenue:
(1) States cannot exclude religious entities from public programs because of their religion.
(2) State governments cannot exclude religious organizations from a student aid program just because the program affords students the choice of attending religious schools.

Free Exercise Clause issues have also arisen regarding church and ministry hiring. Most of the time they involve a religious entity seeking to hire or fire someone based on their religious standards and an employee claiming he or she was discriminated against in the hiring or firing process. Here's what one such case looks like:

Our Lady of Guadalupe School v. Morrissey-Berru (2020)

Agnes Morrissey-Berru was a teacher at Our Lady of Guadalupe School, a Catholic school in Hermosa Beach, California. Her role as a teacher included teaching on religious topics, leading prayer, and otherwise functioning in a religious ministry-related capacity. In 2015, the school chose not to renew her teaching contract after she began exhibiting poor performance as a teacher. She sued, claiming that she had been discriminated against because of her age.

In the 2012 case of *Hosana-Tabor Evangelical Lutheran Church v. Equal Opportunity Employment Commission*, the Supreme Court held that religious entities are protected by the Free Exercise Clause in their decisions to hire or fire ministers. Therefore, the issue in *Morrissey-Berru* came down to whether Agnes Morrissey-Berru was a "minister" in this sense.

The Supreme Court held that she was a "minister" because she had a religious *function* that involved significant religious responsibilities. Therefore, the school was protected by the Free Exercise Clause in its decision not to renew her contract.

Key Takeaway from Our Lady of Guadalupe School v. Morrissey-Berru:
(1) Religious groups can only operate freely if they have full freedom to choose and remove those who teach their beliefs. Therefore, the government cannot control a church or religious school's decision about who teaches its religious beliefs. This is known as the "ministerial exception." It reflects the fact that, in many cases, religious faith and education go hand-in-hand.
(2) Whether someone is a "minister" depends on function, not title or status.

Finally, there is the *Little Sisters* case. This case has been bouncing around the federal courts for nearly a decade.

Little Sisters of the Poor v. Pennsylvania (2020)

The Affordable Care Act (ACA) required that women's health insurance include coverage for contraception. In 2017, the Trump administration gave religious entities an exemption from this mandate. The Little Sisters of the Poor, an organization of Catholic nuns, used this exemption to avoid violating their religious beliefs against the use of contraceptives. Pennsylvania sued the federal government, arguing that the Trump administration's exemption was unlawful.

The Supreme Court upheld the exemption. The Court stated that RFRA supported the exemption and that states cannot second-guess the validity of a person's religious beliefs.

Key Takeaway from Little Sisters of the Poor v. Pennsylvania:
(1) A religious exemption from the Affordable Care Act's contraception coverage requirement is valid under RFRA.

SUMMING IT ALL UP

(1) The framers protected religious exercise because they recognized that religion cultivates the kind of virtue that is necessary for the success of the republic.
(2) The *Smith* decision continues to be controversial because it potentially allows state governments to require people to violate their religious beliefs. It is balanced out by the federal RFRA and the many states that have their own RFRA.
(3) The "ministerial exception" says that religious groups must be free to choose their leaders without government interference.
(4) *Trinity Lutheran* and *Espinoza* establish the same principle: states cannot exclude religious entities from public programs because of their religion.

THINGS TO THINK ABOUT

(1) Over time, there has been an increase in efforts to pit the two religion clauses against each other. Many states are now arguing that a law that infringes on free exercise rights is necessary to prevent an establishment of religion. In other words, they try to use the Establishment Clause to fend off the Free Exercise Clause. You can probably see how these efforts are a result of the false notion that the Establishment Clause creates a "wall of separation" between church and state (Chapter 12). If one believes that there must be a wall of separation between church and state, one can justify nearly any burden on religious exercise.

(2) Recent years have seen a sharp increase in challenges to religious liberty. *Masterpiece Cakeshop v Colorado Civil Rights Commission*, which involved a Christian baker who refused on religious grounds to bake a wedding cake for a homosexual couple, was the most high-profile of these cases, but there are many more. One primary cause is the increase in suits against religious persons by LGBTQ individuals or advocacy groups who see religious beliefs and religious individuals as bigoted. Others claim that religion is an excuse for violating civil rights.

(3) Is irreligion (or non-religion) now the Supreme Court's preferred constitutional value?

(4) *Smith* held that the government has no duty to provide religious exemptions from laws that apply neutrally to everyone. But is there such a thing as a neutral law? Will any law ever apply to all people and all religious faiths in a completely neutral way?

(5) *Little Sisters of the Poor* is a very strange case, if you think about it. A *state* government sued the *federal* government to force it to require *Catholic nuns* to distribute contraceptives. Are Catholic nuns necessary for implementing the ACA?

CHAPTER 14: FREE SPEECH

Why would the Constitution protect free speech?

Because speech is a central part of what makes us human. Speech is how we make sense of the world; it enables us to create meaning and order out of chaos. It is the ultimate free act.

The framers recognized this, given their ancestors' experiences under European regimes in which citizens could not speak their minds without fear of punishment. They understood that the ability to speak freely was one of the most important and foundational freedoms of all.

We'll dive into the cases in a minute, but there are two things you need to know before we do.

First, speech can include things that don't involve speaking. Actions can count as speech. For instance, waving a banner with a political message on it counts as speech. We call this kind of speech "expressive conduct" because, while not physical speech, it is expressing a message through conduct.

Second, there are certain kinds of speech that are not protected. They include (but are not limited to):
(1) Speech advocating imminent lawlessness (illegal activity that is about to happen *right now*)
(2) Fighting words (words that would cause a violent response in the listener)
(3) Obscenity (words that are not tolerated by standards of decency in a civilized society)
(4) False/deceptive advertising
(5) Defamation (public speech about another person that is false and damages his reputation)

The Free Speech Clause has, like most of the other provisions in the Bill of Rights, been applied to the states as well as the federal government. Here are some of the most important Free Speech Clause cases.

West Virginia State Board of Education v. Barnette (1943) (*"the pledge case"*)

The West Virginia State Board of Education required public-school teachers and students to salute the flag using the pledge of allegiance. The Barnette family, who were Jehovah's Witnesses, refused to perform the pledge of allegiance because their religion forbade them from saluting symbols. The Barnette children were sent home from school for not participating in the pledge of allegiance. They sued, arguing that the compulsory pledge of allegiance violated the First Amendment's protections of free speech.

The Supreme Court held that the Board of Education's pledge of allegiance requirement was unconstitutional. The government cannot force an opinion on anyone, including allegiance to the flag of the United States.

Key Takeaway from West Virginia State Board of Education v. Barnette:
(1) The Free Speech Clause means that the government cannot force an opinion on any citizen.

Wooley v. Maynard (1977) (*"the license plate case"*)
New Hampshire law required all license plates to show the state motto: "Live Free or Die." George Maynard, a Jehovah's Witness, refused to comply with this law based on his religious beliefs. He challenged the law as a violation of free speech. The Supreme Court held that the New Hampshire law unconstitutionally interfered with the freedom of speech.

Key Takeaway from Wooley v. Maynard:
(1) Requiring citizens to use their private property as a "mobile billboard" for the state's message violated the Free Speech Clause of the First Amendment.

Texas v. Johnson (1989) (*"the flag burning case"*)
Gregory Johnson set an American flag on fire in front of the Dallas city hall. He was convicted under a Texas law that prohibited burning the American flag. Johnson challenged his conviction, arguing that flag-burning is a form of expressive conduct that is protected by the Free Speech Clause. Texas argued in return that the flag was a symbol of national unity that should not be destroyed.

The Supreme Court held that flag-burning is a form of expressive conduct that is protected by the Free Speech Clause. The following quote from the Court sums it up: "If there is a bedrock principle underlying the First Amendment, it is that the Government may not prohibit the expression of an idea simply because society finds the idea itself offensive or disagreeable."

Key Takeaways from Texas v. Johnson:
(1) Flag-burning is a form of expressive conduct that is protected by the Free Speech Clause.
(2) The government cannot prohibit the expression of an idea just because society doesn't like the idea.

RAV v. City of St. Paul (1992)

A group of teenagers burned a cross on a black family's lawn and were charged under a local ordinance prohibiting the display of symbols that "arouse anger, alarm or resentment in others on the basis of race, color, creed, religion or gender." The teenagers challenged this ordinance as an improper restriction on their free speech right to express their beliefs.

The Supreme Court agreed with them. The ordinance violated the Free Speech Clause because it prohibited speech on the basis of its content. The government cannot punish speech or expressive conduct just because it disagrees with the ideas that are being expressed, even where (as in this case) the ideas are extremely violent and traumatizing.

*Just to be clear: burning a cross on someone's lawn can (and obviously should) be punished. The point of this case is only that the government can't punish it on Free Speech grounds.

Key Takeaway from RAV v. City of St. Paul:
(1) The government cannot punish speech or expressive conduct just because it disagrees with the ideas that are being expressed.

Citizens United v. Federal Election Commission (2010)

A political advocacy non-profit called Citizens United wanted to show a film criticizing presidential candidate Hillary Clinton before the 2008 Democratic primary elections. The Bipartisan Campaign Reform Act of 2002, however, prohibited them from doing so. This statute prohibited any corporation from making an "electioneering communication" within 30 days of a primary election. Citizens United sued the Federal Election Commission (FEC), arguing that the Act violated the First Amendment's protections of free speech.

The Supreme Court held that the Act was unconstitutional. Prohibiting corporations from spending their money toward a political cause violated the First Amendment's protections of free speech. This is because corporations are considered legal persons.

Key Takeaway from Citizens United v. Federal Election Commission:
(1) Political spending by corporations – which are considered legal persons – is a form of protected speech under the First Amendment.

SUMMING IT ALL UP

(1) The Free Speech Clause is powerful, and it protects a lot of expression that many people would find harmful and offensive.
(2) Requiring citizens to use their private property as a "mobile billboard" for the state's message violated the Free Speech Clause of the First Amendment.
(3) The government cannot punish speech or expressive conduct just because it disagrees with the ideas that are being expressed. It also can't punish speech just because society doesn't like that speech.
(4) Political spending by corporations, associations, and labor unions is a form of protected speech under the First Amendment.

THINGS TO THINK ABOUT

(1) Notice how similar the Free Speech cases are to many of the cases that deal with religion. Remember *American Legion* (the case about the WWI memorial cross)? The Court concluded in that case that merely being offended by a religiously affiliated symbol doesn't mean that you have an Establishment Clause claim. Likewise, many of the Free Speech cases show that speech cannot be banned just because it may be disagreeable. In both instances, the American tradition is to allow a wide berth for free speech and free religious expression.

(2) Over time, we can see a shift toward relativism in the Free Speech Clause cases. Relativism is the idea that there is no objective truth. Cases like *R.A.V. v. St. Paul* and *Texas v. Johnson* proceed on the assumption that all speech is valid, even if is offensive, unpatriotic, or potentially dangerous. Whether this trend is a good thing or not is up to you, but it's worth pointing out. If relativism is the new standard, is there any point to political debate? Relativism is also related to the "fake news" phenomenon, in which both sides of the political divide accuse the other side of publishing and relying on false facts. But in a relativistic society in which there are no objective truths, do we even have a basis for objecting to anyone's preferred facts?

(3) *Citizens United* continues to be very controversial. Supporters of this decision argue that it preserves the right to participate in political advocacy, regardless of whether one is acting in a personal or corporate capacity. Opponents say that it allows special interests to have too much political clout. What do you think?

(4) *Texas v. Johnson* is difficult to reconcile with a sense of patriotism. Do we really want people burning the flag? What about the fact that both flag-burning is fundamentally anti-American?

CHAPTER 15: GUNS

You've probably heard the phrase "right to bear arms" before. This phrase refers to the Second Amendment, which primarily protects the right to bear arms.

The following cases show where the Second Amendment currently lies. They also provide an interesting review of the incorporation process, which is the process by which the Supreme Court has gradually applied the Bill of Rights to the states (remember: they originally only applied to the federal government). You may remember from Chapter 11 that the Court does this incorporation process through the Fourteenth Amendment's Due Process Clause. If the right in question is "fundamental" or "deeply rooted in this Nation's history and tradition," it is applied to the states.

District of Columbia v. Heller (2008)

The District of Columbia banned handguns. Dick Heller, a District of Columbia police officer who was authorized to carry a handgun while on duty, was denied a handgun license under this rule. He sued the District of Columbia, arguing that the handgun ban violated the Second Amendment's right to bear arms.

The Supreme Court held that the handgun ban violated the Second Amendment. *Heller* confirmed the right to keep and use arms for self-defense and other lawful purposes.

The Second Amendment applied in this case because the law was enacted in the District of Columbia, which is a federal enclave (not a state). The Court did not address whether the Second Amendment also applied to the states. That happened a few years later in *McDonald v. City of Chicago*.

Key Takeaway from District of Columbia v. Heller:
(1) The Second Amendment protects the right to own arms (weapons such as firearms) for personal use.

McDonald v. City of Chicago (2010)

The city of Chicago, Illinois banned the possession of handguns. Otis McDonald and several other Chicago residents argued that the ban violated the Second Amendment. The only problem for McDonald and the other plaintiffs was that, as you remember from *Heller*, the Second Amendment hadn't been applied to the states yet. It only applied to the federal government. So McDonald had to argue that the Second Amendment should be applied to the states.

The Supreme Court held that the Second Amendment applied to the states through the Due Process Clause of the Fourteenth Amendment because it was "fundamental" and "deeply rooted" in American history. Therefore, the Chicago ordinance was unconstitutional.

Key Takeaway from McDonald v. City of Chicago:
(1) The Second Amendment applies to the states.

SUMMING IT ALL UP

(1) The Second Amendment, which now applies to the states as well as the federal government, protects the right to keep and use arms (weapons such as firearms) for self-defense and other lawful purposes.

THINGS TO THINK ABOUT

(1) This is obviously a very controversial issue. As a matter of original meaning, it is clear that the framers intended to protect the right to keep and use firearms. However, pressure is mounting during the modern era to reconsider this protection. There is a lot of debate about how far this right extends. How would you resolve this debate?

CHAPTER 16: SEARCH & SEIZE

It's time for some Law & Order.

We are now entering the criminal law portion of the Constitution.

This chapter will focus on the Fourth Amendment, which protects you from unreasonable searches and seizures (arrests). It also requires that search or arrest warrants (1) be based on Probable Cause and (2) describe the place to be searched or the items to be seized.

As always, there is one big concept that you need to understand before we look at the cases: the difference between Probable Cause and Reasonable Suspicion. Think about them as justifications. If your employer accuses you of neglecting your job duties, your natural inclination is (after you apologize, of course) to offer an explanation for your conduct. In other words, you try to show why you had good reason to act the way you did. You offer a *justification* for your actions. Probable Cause and Reasonable Suspicion operate the same way. They are justifications that the police must have in order to stop, search, or arrest you.

Reasonable Suspicion is what the police must have in order to stop you. You've probably heard the term "Stop & Frisk." The "stop" portion requires the officer to have *reasonable suspicion* that a crime has been or will be committed. If they have reasonable suspicion, they can stop you and do a limited search for weapons or other illegal activity.

Probable Cause, on the other hand, is what the police must have in order to search or arrest you (or to get a warrant to do those things). Since arresting is more serious than just stopping, Probable Cause requires more than Reasonable Suspicion does. Probable Cause requires that the officers have sufficient facts to believe that the suspect has committed a crime (for an arrest) or that items related to criminal activity will be found at a particular place (for a search).

SEARCHES

Here are some prominent cases that involved the Fourth Amendment's prohibition on unreasonable searches and seizures.

Katz v. United States (1967) ("*the phone booth case*")
Federal agents suspected Charles Katz of running an illegal gambling scheme. To get evidence on him, they attached an eavesdropping device to outside of a public phone booth that he regularly used. Using this device, they recorded his phone conversations and confirmed that he was running an illegal gambling scheme.

Katz argued that the recordings of his phone conversations should not be allowed into evidence because a person has an expectation of privacy once they enter a phone booth. The government responded that since the device had been placed on the outside of the phone booth, there was no invasion of privacy.

The Supreme Court held that the federal agents violated the Fourth Amendment's protection against unreasonable searches by listening to his phone booth conversations without a warrant. This is because a person has a reasonable expectation of privacy in a phone booth.

Key Takeaways from Katz v. United States:
(1) The Fourth Amendment's protections can apply to your home *and* places outside it.
(2) A police action becomes a Fourth Amendment search that requires a warrant if it violates a reasonable expectation of privacy.

United States v. Jones (2011) (*"the nightclub case"*)
Antoine Jones owned a nightclub in Washington, D.C. The police suspected that Jones was trafficking drugs through the nightclub. They obtained a search warrant to place a GPS tracker on Jones' car. They used the tracker to document his movement for four consecutive weeks. The information they gathered from the GPS tracker confirmed that Jones was trafficking drugs.

Jones argued that the evidence gathered by the GPS tracker should not be admitted into evidence because the police violated his Fourth Amendment protection against unreasonable searches. The Supreme Court agreed – the police had violated Jones' Fourth Amendment rights because they had trespassed on what the Fourth Amendment calls his "personal effects."

Key Takeaway from United States v. Jones:
(1) The Fourth Amendment is implicated if the police trespass on someone's property for the purpose of obtaining information.

Katz and *Jones* provide two different tests for determining whether there has been a Fourth Amendment search that requires a warrant. Which do you think is the better test?

SEIZURES

"Seizure" is another word for an arrest. Seizures require Probable Cause.

United States v. Mendenhall (1980) (*"the airport case"*)

When Sylvia Mendenhall arrived at the Detroit airport, police officers noticed that she had different names on her ticket and ID card. The officers asked Mendenhall to accompany them to their office for questioning, and she agreed. She also agreed to a search of her purse and a strip search of her person by a female officer. The search revealed packages of heroin in her undergarments. The question for the Supreme Court was whether this stop and search violated the Fourth Amendment.

The Court said that it did not because Mendenhall had not been seized. She had been searched in a public place (airport), the police officers had politely asked her for permission, and she had voluntarily agreed. A reasonable person in those circumstances would have believed she was free to leave.

Key Takeaway from United States v. Mendenhall:
(1) A person is seized if a reasonable person under the circumstances would believe that he was not free to leave.

STOP & FRISK

Stops & Frisks require Reasonable Suspicion.

Terry v. Ohio (1968)

Police officer Martin McFadden was on duty in downtown Cleveland when he saw three men walking around a department store. He was concerned that they were scouting the store in preparation for a robbery. He asked the men what they were doing. When they didn't answer, he patted them down (otherwise known as "frisking" them) and found pistols in their jackets. He immediately arrested them.

One of them, John Terry, was later convicted of carrying a concealed weapon. He argued that the pistol should be excluded from evidence because the frisk done by Officer McFadden was an unreasonable search that violated the Fourth Amendment. He claimed the arrest was also unreasonable because Officer McFadden did not have reason to believe that Terry was doing something wrong.

The Supreme Court held that both the search and the seizure were reasonable because Officer McFadden had "reasonable suspicion" that the men were armed.

Key Takeaways from Terry v. Ohio:
(1) An officer can "stop" a person if he has "reasonable suspicion" that a crime has been or will be committed.
(2) After an officer stops a person, he is permitted to "frisk" them if he has "reasonable suspicion" that the person is armed and dangerous. A frisk is less than a full search.

SUMMING IT ALL UP

(1) Searches and Seizures (Arrests) require Probable Cause. Stops & Frisks require Reasonable Suspicion. Reasonable Suspicion is a lower standard than Probable Cause.
(2) The Fourth Amendment applies to your home *and* places outside your home.
(3) There are 2 tests you can use to determine if the Fourth Amendment applies to a search:
a. *Katz* test: A search violates the Fourth Amendment if it invades a reasonable expectation of privacy.
b. *Jones* test: A search violates the Fourth Amendment if the police trespass on someone's property for the purpose of obtaining information.
(4) A person is seized if a reasonable person under the circumstances would believe that he was not free to leave.
(5) An officer can "stop" a person if he has "reasonable suspicion" that a crime has been or will be committed. After an officer stops and questions a person, he is permitted to "frisk" them if they have "reasonable suspicion" that the person is armed and dangerous.

THINGS TO THINK ABOUT

(1) Is the *Katz* test or the *Jones* test better for evaluating the legality of searches? Why?

(2) Is Reasonable Suspicion a legitimate standard? It's nowhere in the Fourth Amendment, and there is no evidence suggesting that the original meaning of the Fourth Amendment included Reasonable Suspicion. The Supreme Court seems to have just made it up. Is that ok?

(3) Does the Constitution refer to a "reasonable expectation of privacy"? If not, is the *Katz* test legitimate?

CHAPTER 17: PLEADING THE FIFTH

You've probably heard the phrase "pleading the fifth" before.

But do you know what it means? What about the "Miranda rights"? Many people can recite the Miranda rights from memory. Any idea what they're for? This chapter will explain all of that.

PRIVILEGE AGAINST SELF-INCRIMINATION

This part of the Fifth Amendment says that no one can be forced to testify against themselves. In other words, the government can't force you to be a witness against yourself. This is where we get the phrase "plead the fifth." When you plead the fifth, you are essentially saying, "I want to use my Fifth Amendment right to not have to say anything else."

INTERROGATION RIGHTS

What is an interrogation? It is an interview in which the police try to get information from a suspect. If the police say or do something that they should know is probably going to get the suspect to confess, an interrogation has occurred.

Here's the actual case behind the famous "Miranda rights":

Miranda v. Arizona (1966)

Ernesto Miranda was arrested because the police suspected that he had kidnapped and raped a young girl. He was then interrogated. After two hours of questioning, he confessed to the kidnapping and rape. At trial, Miranda argued that his confession should not be admitted into evidence because he had not been told what his rights were before his interrogation.

The Supreme Court held that the Fifth Amendment requires police officers to advise suspects of their rights before interrogating a person who is in police custody. This is a very famous case because it led to what we now know as the "Miranda rights":

If a person in custody is to be subjected to interrogation, he must first be informed in clear and unequivocal terms that:
- He has a right to remain silent.
- Anything he says can and will be used against him in court.
- He has a right to an attorney (before interrogation and during interrogation), and if he can't afford an attorney, one will be appointed for him.

CHAPTER 18: TAKINGS

There is one more part of the Fifth Amendment that we need to study: the Takings Clause.

This clause says that the government cannot take your private property "for public use" without giving you "just compensation." In other words, they can't confiscate your house without paying you the fair market value of your house.

This part of the Fifth Amendment is concerned with protecting private property. Why would the framers desire to protect private property? Because when property is unprotected, progress halts. When your property can be taken away from you at any moment, you are forced to spend all your time protecting what you have rather than innovating or developing new ideas. In early societies where kings and warlords could take their subjects' land whenever they pleased, innovation and economic growth were at a standstill. Once property rights became secure, innovation and economic growth took off because people weren't spending all their time worrying about losing what they had. The bottom line: protecting private property is necessary because insecure property rights stifles innovation and stops progress.

There are two kinds of takings: *physical* and *regulatory*.

A physical taking is what it sounds like: the government taking your physical property.

A regulatory taking is less obvious. It occurs where a government regulation or law limits your use of your property in a way that deprives you of your property's value. For example, consider a law that prohibits landowners from building additional dwellings (in addition to their own home) on their property. If you wanted to build a second house on your property to rent for some extra income, the law would prohibit you from doing so. This might be considered a regulatory taking because the law has deprived you of the value of your own property. It has removed your ability to make a profit from your own property.

Here is a case that deals with regulatory takings:

Kelo v. New London (2005)
The town of New London, Connecticut was struggling. In order to improve the economy, the town decided to buy property and transfer it to the pharmaceutical company Pfizer. Pfizer planned to build a new research facility in New London that would hopefully bring in jobs and revenue.

One of the homes the town tried to purchase belonged to Susette Kelo. Kelo refused to sell and filed suit, arguing that this was a taking that was not for a "public use" because her property would be sold to Pfizer, a private company. Did the town violate the Fifth Amendment's Takings Clause by taking her private property and selling it to a private corporation?

In one of its most controversial opinions, the Supreme Court held that the town had *not* violated the Fifth Amendment's Takings Clause. In other words, taking Kelo's property and selling it to Pfizer *was* a "public use." This was because the town was taking the land with the ultimate goal of benefiting the town economically. That was enough to constitute a "public use."

The Pfizer facility was never built. Kelo's lot remains vacant to this day.

Key Takeaway from Kelo v. New London:
(1) The town did not violate the Fifth Amendment's Takings Clause by taking Kelo's private property and selling it to a private corporation because the taking was done with the ultimate goal of benefiting the entire town.

SUMMING IT ALL UP

(1) The Takings Clause says that the government cannot take your private property "for public use" without giving you "just compensation."
(2) There are two kinds of takings: *physical* and *regulatory*.
(3) There is no bright-line rule for regulatory takings cases. Each case depends on its particular facts and circumstances.

THINGS TO THINK ABOUT

(1) What do you think of the government's actions in *Kelo*? Is selling someone's home to a private company a "public use" just because you're hoping the end result will benefit everyone?
(2) The question remains: how much can the government burden a property owner before it must pay the owner "just compensation"?

CHAPTER 19: CRUEL AND UNUSUAL

The Eighth Amendment prohibits three things: (1) excessive bail, (2) excessive fines, and (3) cruel and unusual punishments.

Bail is the process by which you pay a certain amount of money to be released from police custody. The Eighth Amendment prohibits courts from setting the bail amount excessively high.
The same is true for fines. The Eighth Amendment prohibits courts and governments from imposing excessively large fines.

The cruel and unusual punishments portion is the most well-known part of the Eighth Amendment. What kinds of punishments are considered "cruel and unusual"? Is a life prison sentence for a parking violation "cruel and unusual"?

We don't know much about the Eighth Amendment, so we lack an answer to many of these questions. However, we do know that the "cruel and unusual punishments" language was based on similar language in the English Bill of Rights. We also know that the American people must have felt that it was a serious enough issue to warrant a constitutional amendment of its own!

Perhaps the biggest controversy regarding the Eighth Amendment is whether the death penalty is "cruel and unusual." Many have argued that it is and should therefore be illegal. *Gregg v. Georgia* weighed in on this question in 1976.

Gregg v. Georgia (1976) (*"the death penalty case"*)

Troy Gregg was found guilty of armed robbery and murder. He was sentenced to death. Gregg challenged his sentence, arguing that the death penalty was "cruel and unusual punishment" that violated the Eighth Amendment.

The Supreme Court disagreed. It held that the death penalty is not cruel and unusual punishment for crimes as serious as intentional murder. The fact that a majority of the states have death penalty statutes shows that the American people have not decided that the death penalty needs to be outlawed. In addition, the Fifth Amendment lays out procedures for capital punishment; why would it do so if the Constitution did not assume that the death penalty was valid?

Key Takeaway from Gregg v. Georgia:
(1) The death sentence is not "cruel and unusual punishment" for the crime of intentional murder.

SUMMING IT ALL UP

(1) The Eighth Amendment prohibits three things: (1) excessive bail, (2) excessive fines, and (3) cruel and unusual punishments.
(2) The Supreme Court has held that a death sentence for the crime of murder is not "cruel and unusual punishment."

CHAPTER 20: INK BLOT

At his U.S. Supreme Court confirmation hearing, Judge Robert Bork was asked by Arizona Senator Dennis DeConcini about the meaning of the Ninth Amendment. This was his response:

> "I do not think you can use the Ninth Amendment unless you know something of what it means. For example, if you had an amendment that says 'Congress shall make no' and then there is an ink blot and you cannot read the rest of it and that is the only copy you have, I do not think the court can make up what might be under the ink blot if you cannot read it."

An ink blot.

That is what we've come to see the Ninth Amendment as.

And for good reason. It is incredibly confusing: "The enumeration in the Constitution, of certain rights, shall not be construed to deny or disparage others retained by the people." Huh?

When the Constitution was being drafted, there was a lot of concern about whether a national Constitution would deprive the individual states of their independence. James Madison, one of the writers of the Constitution, proposed the Ninth Amendment as a way to assure the states that the proposed national Constitution would not harm or take away the rights that the states had already established in their individual state constitutions. You'll often hear the argument that the Ninth Amendment protects rights that aren't in the Constitution. That is true – but not so that judges can make up new rights. It is true because it protects the rights in the state constitutions, many of which are not in the U.S. Constitution.

In this sense, the Ninth Amendment is all about federalism. Federalism, you'll remember from Chapter 2, is the division of power between the states and the federal government. The Ninth Amendment was meant to protect the states from federal interference. That is the essence of federalism.

What is the key concept you should remember about the Ninth Amendment? That it is not a repository of every imaginable right, but rather a protection of the states from federal power.

CHAPTER 21: FEDERALISM

It may not have been apparent right away, but we now know that the Ninth Amendment is all about federalism.

As it turns out, so is the Tenth Amendment.

The Tenth Amendment says that the federal government only has what the Constitution gives it. *Everything else* is for the states. This reflects the framers' intention that the United States be a country governed from the ground up (by the people), not the top down (by the federal government or a king).

Hammer v. Dagenhart (1918) (*"the child labor case"*)

Congress passed the Keating-Owen Child Labor Act to prohibit the interstate shipment of goods produced by child labor. Fourteen-year-old Rueben Dagenhart's father filed suit, arguing that the law restricted his freedom to have Rueben work in a textile factory.

The Supreme Court held that the Act was invalid under the Tenth Amendment because it regulated production (one of the states' powers) rather than commerce (one of Congress' powers). The Constitution does not give the federal government the power to regulate production – only commerce. By trying to regulate production rather than commerce, the law invaded the powers that were reserved for the states.

Key Takeaway from Hammer v. Dagenhart:
(1) The Constitution gives Congress the ability to regulate commerce, not production. Regulating production is for the states. Therefore, a federal act regulating production is invalid.

New York v. United States (1992) & Printz v. United States (1997)

Congress created an incentive program for states to safely dispose of radioactive waste. If a state was unable to dispose of the waste, it had to take ownership of the waste. The state of New York challenged this law, arguing that Congress could not force the states to do this. The Supreme Court held that the incentive program violated the Tenth Amendment because it forced the state governments to serve a federal government purpose.

Congress enacted the Brady Handgun Violence Prevention Act in 1993. The law proposed a national background-check database for firearm dealers. While the database was being built, the Act commanded local sheriffs around the country to conduct background checks on people buying firearms. Sheriff Jay Printz challenged this law, arguing that the federal government could not force local law enforcement officials to take action in this way. The Supreme Court agreed – Congress cannot force state officials to serve a federal government purpose.

Key Takeaway from New York v. United States & Printz v. United States:

76

(1) Congress cannot force the states to serve a federal government purpose.

SUMMING IT ALL UP

(1) Congress cannot force the states to serve a federal government purpose.
(2) The federal government only has what the Constitution gives it. *Everything else* is for the states.

CHAPTER 22: SOVEREIGN IMMUNITY

After the previous two chapters, we know that the Ninth and Tenth Amendment are all about federalism. They limit the federal government's ability to overpower the states.

The Eleventh Amendment, on the other hand, focuses on the states. It originally prohibited citizens from suing other states. For instance, if you lived in Arkansas, you were prohibited by the Eleventh Amendment from suing the state of Montana. Eventually, the Eleventh Amendment was expanded to include suits against your own state. Now, if you live in Arkansas, you are prohibited from suing the state of Montana *as well as* the state of Arkansas.

This concept is called Sovereign Immunity. Here's an example of how it works in real life:

Hans v. State of Louisiana (1890)
    The state of Louisiana failed to pay interest on certain bonds. Hans, a Louisiana citizen, sued the state of Louisiana to force it to pay its debts. Louisiana argued that Hans could not sue the state because of the state's sovereign immunity.
    The Supreme Court agreed with the state of Louisiana. Hans could not sue Louisiana to force it to pay its debts unless the state consented to being sued.

Key Takeaways from Hans v. Louisiana:
(1) After *Hans*, individuals were prohibited from suing other states *and* their own state.

(2) An individual citizen cannot sue his own state unless the state consents to be sued.

SUMMING IT ALL UP

(1) The Eleventh Amendment bars states from being sued by individual citizens. This means that you cannot sue your home state. It also means that you cannot sue any other state.

CHAPTER 23: THE ELECTORAL COLLEGE

Article II and the Twelfth Amendment lay out the process for electing the President. You probably know the citizens' role in that process: voting. But there's also another part: the Electoral College.

The Electoral College is composed of "electors" from each state. Each state gets a number of electors equal to its total number of representatives in Congress (senators + representatives). After the national popular vote is cast, the Electors meet and vote for the President and the Vice President. The candidate who receives the majority of the Electors' votes wins the election.

Why do we have the Electoral College? When the framers were trying to figure out how to elect the president, they had two options: (1) a national popular vote or (2) a vote by the members of Congress. The national popular vote enabled the people to participate, but the framers were worried about a national popular vote devolving into mob rule, like it had in Ancient Greece. They therefore created the Electoral College as a compromise that would allow the people to vote, ensure fairness between the states, and check public passions.

What are the benefits of the Electoral College? First, it protects the ability of each state to participate and ensures that bigger states (which have more representatives in Congress) don't overpower the smaller states. In this way, the Electoral College protects political minorities. Second, it discourages voter fraud. A national popular vote system would inevitably lead to a race to the bottom, with both parties doing whatever it took (lowering the voting age to 14, letting prisoners vote, promoting violence, fabricating votes, etc.) to get more votes. Third, it ensures that the President makes his case to people from all parts of the country. If we had a national popular vote system, presidential candidates could just focus on the biggest cities with the most voting power. But the Electoral College forces them to appeal to big cities and small towns alike.

There have recently been many proposals to get rid of the Electoral College. One of these proposals is based on the argument that the Electoral College was designed to perpetuate slavery. It says that because the Electoral College let the southern states count their slaves for purposes of selecting electors back in the 1800s, the southern states were able to get extra electors. Since the Electoral College let the slave-holding states gain more power, so the argument goes, the whole Electoral College should be scrapped. But this argument forgets two very important things. First is the fact that in 1787, when the Constitution was being written, slavery was practiced in *all* the states. So any benefit for the southern slave-holding states was given to the northern non-slave-holding states as well. Second is the fact that the Electoral College actually contributed to *ending* slavery! Abraham Lincoln would not have been elected had it not been for the Electoral College. He received only 39% of the popular vote, but he won by a large margin in the Electoral College. In this way, the Electoral College helped to end slavery, not perpetuate it.

THINGS TO THINK ABOUT

(1) What do you think of the idea of doing away with the Electoral College? Would getting rid of the Electoral College change anything about what happened in the past?

(2) Would a switch to a pure popular vote be a good thing? Or would it expose us to changing social passions and make our elections meaningless? Would it mean that billionaires could buy elections?

CHAPTER 24: THE THIRTEENTH AMENDMENT

In 1864, Congress voted to add the Thirteenth Amendment to the Constitution. This amendment permanently abolished slavery in the United States.

The amendment was very controversial at the time. The Republicans and President Abraham Lincoln supported the amendment, but the Democrats insisted that the amendment was unconstitutional. They argued incorrectly that the Constitution protected slavery. Thankfully, they did not prevail. The ideals of the Declaration of Independence did.

The language in the Thirteenth Amendment was copied from the 1787 Northwest Ordinance, which banned slavery in the Northwest Territory. And the Northwest Ordinance was written by the very same man who wrote the Declaration of Independence: Thomas Jefferson. In other words, the words that abolished slavery came from the same exact source as the words that forever committed America to fighting the evils of slavery: "all men are created equal." As Martin Luther King, Jr. would say many years later, the Thirteenth Amendment was the fulfillment of the promise of the Declaration of Independence.

The framers of the Constitution were very clear about their opposition to slavery, which – at the time – existed in nearly every society on earth. Thomas Jefferson said that slavery was "at war with the concepts of our country" and denounced slavery in his famous *Notes on the State of Virginia.* Alexander Hamilton said that emancipating the slaves was required by "the dictates of humanity." James Madison called slavery "the most oppressive dominion ever exercised." Benjamin Franklin called slavery "an atrocious debasement of human nature." John Adams repeatedly said that slavery should be abolished from the United States, calling it a "foul contagion" and an "evil of colossal magnitude." Even Alexander Stephens, vice president of the Confederacy, understood that the framers believed that "the enslavement of the African was in violation of the laws of nature; that it was wrong in principle, socially, morally, and politically."

Slavery was a big issue during the framing of the Constitution. The southern states and the Democrats supported slavery; the northern states and the Republicans opposed it. The southern states said that they would not join the union if slavery was not included. In addition, the southern states wanted to count their slaves as part of their population total so that they could get more representatives in Congress. (The number of representatives a state has is based on its population, so the larger your population, the more representatives you get. This was just a power play by the southern states).

The framers were therefore faced with a nearly impossible dilemma. On one hand, they could allow the southern states to continue owning slaves and have one union. On the other hand, they could forbid slavery, lose the entire union, and give the southern states complete freedom to expand slavery as much as they wanted. Behind all of this was their fear that America might go the way of Haiti, where whites and blacks slaughtered each other in a vicious race war from 1791-1804.

They did two things to solve this problem.

First, they agreed to the Three-Fifths Compromise, which allowed the southern states to count their slaves as three-fifths of a person for purposes of representation in Congress. Contrary to popular opinion, therefore, the Three-Fifths Compromise was actually a victory for the northern states because it prevented the southern states from gaining too much power in Congress. If the southern states had been allowed to count their slaves in their population total, they would have gained so much power in Congress that they might have been able to keep slavery indefinitely. It is important to note that the Three-Fifths Compromise was *not* because the northern states saw slaves as less than human. They saw them as fully human, but in order to prevent the southern states from bolstering their power and potentially protecting slavery for many years to come, they had to create a temporary compromise.

Second, they made sure that the Constitution and other founding documents (1) did not condone or even mention slavery and (2) provided the principles that would eventually lead to the abolishment of slavery. That is why neither the Declaration of Independence nor the Constitution contain any endorsement of slavery: so that slavery would be put on the path to what President Abraham Lincoln called "ultimate extinction." Frederick Douglass recognized this: "Abolish slavery tomorrow, and not a sentence or syllable of the Constitution need be altered." The framers explicitly based the republic on the concept of legal equality, trusting in future generations to fulfill that promise.

They were right to do so. President Abraham Lincoln fulfilled that promise in a big way by emancipating the slaves. The Thirteenth Amendment was another step in that direction. And Martin Luther King, Jr., referred to his efforts during the Civil Rights Movement as another step toward the fulfillment of those great ideals. These heroic leaders didn't run away from the American founding or its ideals of liberty and equality; they ran even harder toward them.

CHAPTER 25: DUE PROCESS – THE SEEDS OF CHANGE

The Constitution has two due process clauses – one in the Fifth Amendment and one in the Fourteenth Amendment.

The Fifth Amendment's Due Process Clause says that the federal government cannot deprive anyone of "life, liberty or property without due process of law." It deals with *procedure*, or methods. It doesn't guarantee any outcomes. **It is all about the process, not the results**. Over time, however, this procedural focus has been eroded in favor of creating results. *Dred Scott* was the start of this process.

Dred Scott v. Sandford (1857)

Dred Scott was a slave in Missouri. He was taken to Illinois (a free state) in 1833, where he resided for ten years. Upon his return to Missouri, his master claimed Scott was still his slave. Scott sued for his freedom. The Supreme Court, in one of its most unfortunate decisions, held in an opinion by Chief Justice Roger Taney that Scott was still a slave because "negro[s], whose ancestors were imported . . . and sold as slaves," could not be free American citizens.

So how did this case deal with the Fifth Amendment's Due Process Clause? Chief Justice Taney used it to support his conclusion. Since the Fifth Amendment's Due Process Clause says that the government cannot deprive a citizen of his or her property without due process of law, Taney reasoned that slaves – which were considered property at that time – could not be taken from their owners without due process of law. In other words, Justice Taney reasoned that declaring Dred Scott a free man would deprive Scott's owner of his property without due process of law.

Chief Justice Taney's use of the Fifth Amendment's Due Process Clause is strange. The clause guarantees due *process* (the procedures that must be used before the government can deprive anyone of their property), but Taney was using it to guarantee a particular *outcome* (the perpetuation of slavery).

Key Takeaways from Dred Scott v. Sandford:
(1) Due to its perpetuation of slavery, this is one of the most shameful decisions in the Supreme Court's history. Thankfully, it was nullified by the passage of the Thirteenth and Fourteenth Amendments.

(2) *Dred Scott* utilized the Fifth Amendment's Due Process Clause. It held that declaring Dred Scott a free man would deprive Scott's owner of his property without due process of law.

(3) *Dred Scott* was the beginning of the erosion of the concept of due process – away from process and toward substance or outcomes. More on this later.

The Fifth Amendment originally applied to the federal government, but it has since been applied to the states as well (see Chapter 11).

* * * * *

Now let's take a look at the Fourteenth Amendment's Due Process Clause. The Fourteenth Amendment's purpose was to provide recently freed black Americans with the same citizenship status as all other Americans. The amendment says that "[n]o State shall . . . deprive any person of life, liberty, or property, without due process of law." Notice the difference between this Due Process Clause and the Fifth Amendment Due Process Clause: it requires the *states* – not the federal government – to provide due process. This is why the Court was able to use it to apply the Bill of Rights to the states.

The Slaughterhouse Cases (1873)

Louisiana gave a market monopoly to a private slaughterhouse called Crescent City Slaughterhouse Company. A group of butchers sued the state, arguing that the monopoly given to Crescent violated the Fourteenth Amendment by depriving them of liberty and property without due process of law.

The Supreme Court held that the monopoly did *not* violate the Due Process Clause of the Fourteenth Amendment. This was because the Fourteenth Amendment was passed with the specific goal of granting full equality to former slaves. It was not passed to protect any and all rights that a citizen may claim.

Justice Stephen Johnson Field wrote a very important dissenting opinion. Field argued that the Fourteenth Amendment did not *just* protect former slaves; it also protected other rights of other people in other contexts. This foreshadowed what the Fourteenth Amendment – and particularly its Due Process Clause – would eventually become.

Key Takeaways from The Slaughterhouse Cases:
(1) A state-granted monopoly to one private slaughterhouse did not violate the Fourteenth Amendment's Due Process Clause because the Fourteenth Amendment was passed with the specific goal of granting full equality to former slaves.
(2) Justice Field's dissent foreshadowed what the Fourteenth Amendment – and particularly its Due Process Clause – would become.

The Civil Rights Cases (1883)

Congress passed the Civil Rights Act of 1875 to affirm the equal ability of all citizens, regardless of race, to enjoy the benefits of society. In five separate cases, a private institution denied a black person access to certain benefits that were available to a white person. When the black individuals sued under the Civil Rights Act of 1875, the establishment owners argued that the Civil Rights Act of 1875 was unconstitutional because it exceeded Congress' legislative power. The Supreme Court consolidated these five cases into *The Civil Rights Cases* in order to examine whether Congress had overstepped its bounds in enacting the Civil Rights Act of 1875.

The Court held that the Civil Rights Act of 1875 was unconstitutional. In other words, regulating private parties in this way violated the Fourteenth Amendment. This is because the Fourteenth Amendment was passed to provide former slaves with the same civil liberties as all other American citizens, not to regulate private entities generally. Sounds a lot like *The Slaughterhouse Cases*, right?

Justice John Harlan dissented to argue exactly what Justice Field had argued in *The Slaughterhouse Cases*. Harlan said that the Fourteenth Amendment shouldn't be limited to protecting the rights of former slaves; it should apply to a wide range of public and private rights. As you will soon see, it didn't take long for this viewpoint to become widely accepted.

Key Takeaways from The Civil Rights Cases:
(1) The Civil Rights Act of 1875 was unconstitutional because it went beyond the scope of the Fourteenth Amendment, which was intended to protect the rights of former slaves.
(2) Justice Harlan's dissent foreshadowed what the Fourteenth Amendment would become.

SUMMING IT ALL UP

(1) Both Due Process Clauses have the same original meaning. They both guarantee due process of law to the American people. They do not guarantee any substantive outcomes. They are all about the process, not the results.
(2) The only difference between the two Due Process Clauses is that the Fifth Amendment originally applied to the federal government while the Fourteenth Amendment has always applied to the states. The Fifth Amendment has since been applied to the states.
(3) *Dred Scott* used the Due Process Clause of the Fifth Amendment to guarantee certain substantive outcomes even though the clause only guarantees process.
(4) Both the *Civil Rights Cases* and the *Slaughterhouse Cases* stated that the Fourteenth Amendment's Due Process Clause was passed only to provide former slaves with the same civil liberties as all other American citizens, not to regulate private entities generally. However, the dissenting opinions in those cases foreshadowed the future of the Due Process Clause as more than just a guarantee of process.

THINGS TO THINK ABOUT

(1) *Dred Scott* clearly departed from the original meaning of the Due Process Clause. It used a process protection to guarantee the Court's preferred outcome. Is this a problem? Why or why not?

CHAPTER 26: DUE PROCESS – ECONOMIC RIGHTS

Now that we've introduced the two Due Process Clauses and seen some indications that they began to change after the Civil War, let's look at the "second era" of Due Process Clause law.

Dred Scott showed us how the Supreme Court began using a guarantee of process to create particular outcomes. It did so by inserting its preferred right *into* one of the three prongs of the Due Process Clause: life, liberty, or property. This enabled it to reason that taking away that right would violate the Due Process Clause. The "second era" of Due Process Clause law is distinct because it began to apply this approach to economic and social issues. *Lochner* was the start of this process:

Lochner v. New York (1905) (*"the bakery case"*)

The state of New York passed a law called the Bakeshop Act. This act forbade bakers from working more than 60 hours per week, or 10 hours per day. Lochner was fined for letting his workers work more than 60 hours per week. He argued that the Bakeshop Act violated the Due Process Clause of the Fourteenth Amendment because it deprived him of his liberty to work as he pleased without due process of law.

The Supreme Court held that the New York law was unconstitutional because it interfered with the "liberty of contract." The Bakeshop Act deprived Lochner of this liberty without due process of law.

This decision is controversial because the Court completely made up the "liberty of contract." By characterizing Lochner's freedom to work as long as he wanted as part of the "liberty" prong of the Due Process Clause, the majority was then able to claim that the Bakeshop Act took away that "liberty" without due process of law.

Key Takeaways from Lochner v. New York:
(1) The Bakeshop Act violated the Due Process Clause of the Fourteenth Amendment because it took away the "liberty of contract" without due process of law.
(2) *Lochner* is a turning point in the story of the Due Process Clause. Whereas *The Slaughterhouse Cases* and *The Civil Rights Cases* had held the Fourteenth Amendment to its original purpose – giving former slaves the full rights of citizenship – *Lochner* began using its Due Process Clause to protect other rights. In this case, that right happened to be a "liberty of contract."

Adkins v. Children's Hospital of D.C. (1923)

Congress enacted a law that guaranteed a minimum wage to women and children in the District of Columbia. Children's Hospital challenged the law, arguing that it violated the Fifth Amendment's Due Process Clause.

The Supreme Court held that the minimum wage law was invalid because it limited the right identified in *Lochner*: the "liberty of contract." Just as it did in *Lochner*, the Court characterized the liberty of contract as part of the "liberty" portion of the Due Process Clause.

There's one other thing to note here. The Court's ruling assumed that this kind of Congressional interference in daily life was not acceptable. In other words, it presumed that employers and employees should be free to contract without these sorts of rules getting in the way. We call this the **Presumption of Liberty**: the presumption that laws restricting liberty are invalid unless the government can prove otherwise.

However, a few of the justices dissented, arguing that Congress *can* create laws to correct problems in society, even if doing so restricts individual liberty. In other words, if Congress felt that wages for women and children were a problem, it should be able to intervene and make a law to fix that problem – regardless of whether doing so interfered with personal liberty. Keep an eye out for the return of this opinion. It won't be long.

Key Takeaway from Adkins v. Children's Hospital of DC:
(1) A federal law guaranteeing minimum wage to women and children in the District of Columbia violated the Due Process Clause of the Fifth Amendment because it interfered with the "liberty of contract."
(2) This case represents the Presumption of Liberty: the presumption that laws restricting individual liberty are invalid.

Meyer v. Nebraska (1923)

Nebraska passed a law prohibiting elementary schools from teaching any language other than English. Meyer was convicted for teaching German at a Lutheran elementary school. He challenged his conviction, arguing that the Nebraska law violated the Fourteenth Amendment's Due Process Clause.

The Supreme Court agreed with Meyer. This time, rather than using the liberty of contract, the Court created a liberty to teach one's children as one sees fit. It characterized that right as part of the "liberty" prong of the Due Process Clause. In this case, it meant that parents had the right to have their children learn German at school.

Key Takeaway from Meyer v. Nebraska:
(1) Also included in the "liberty" prong of the Due Process Clause is a liberty to teach one's children as one sees fit. The Nebraska law was invalidated because it would have taken this right way without due process of law.
(2) The Court was still operating based on the Presumption of Liberty. It struck down a law on the assumption that government should not be able to restrict individual liberty by interfering in daily life.

Nebbia v. New York (1934) (*"the milk case"*)

The state of New York fixed the price of milk at 9 cents per quart. This price-control law was designed to help dairy farmers recover from the Great Depression, but it ended up raising milk prices for everyone. Grocery store owner Leo Nebbia offered his customers a special deal to avoid the higher prices: if they bought two quarts of milk, he would throw in a free loaf of bread. New York charged Nebbia with violating the price-control law, and he challenged the law in court. The question for the Supreme Court was whether the New York price-control law violated the Due Process Clause of the Fourteenth Amendment.

The Supreme Court held that it did not. The state was free to regulate prices in this way. Due process only required that the law be fair and reasonable.

What a huge difference from the previous cases! First, the Court suddenly returned to the original notion of due process as guaranteeing only fair process. It didn't create any rights or insert anything into the Due Process Clause. Second, the Court said that it was acceptable for governments to regulate private economic activity. This is the opposite of the Presumption of Liberty that we saw in the previous few cases. Were things beginning to change?

Key Takeaways from Nebbia v. New York:

(1) Due process only requires that a law be fair and reasonable. New York's price-control was fair and reasonable, so it was allowed to stand. This was a return to the original meaning of the Due Process Clause: a guarantee of process, not outcomes.

(2) It was also the start of a shift in how the Court viewed the role of the government. While it previously operated on the assumption that government should not be in the business of regulating private conduct, it was now beginning to operate on the assumption that government *can* regulate private conduct.

West Coast Hotel v. Parrish (1937)

The state of Washington imposed a minimum wage for women and children. Elsie Parrish, a maid at the West Coast Hotel in Wenatchee, Washington, filed suit when her employer failed to pay her the minimum wage. The hotel owner argued that Washington's minimum wage law violated the Fifth Amendment's Due Process Clause because it deprived him of the liberty of contract (remember *Lochner*?) without due process of law.

The Supreme Court upheld that the Washington minimum wage law. In other words, the law did not deprive the hotel owner of the liberty of contract without due process of law.

Remember *Adkins*, the case about the children's hospital? You may recall that a few of the justices in that case argued that the government had the power to intervene in society to correct problems. After *Parrish*, that position was now in the majority! The Court's upholding of the Washington minimum wage law solidified the idea that the government can intervene in society to correct problems, even if doing so restricts individual liberty. This continued the change that we saw in *Nebbia*. Before this, the government was seen as a necessary evil that was there to protect the "inalienable" rights protected by the Constitution. Now, the government was seen as an active force in society that could intervene in daily life to fix problems. This view led to the **Presumption of Constitutionality**: the assumption that a law is valid unless proven otherwise. No longer did the government have to justify its intrusions on daily life; now it was the individual who had to show why the government action was invalid.

Key Takeaways from West Coast Hotel v. Parrish:

(1) Washington's minimum wage law did *not* violate the Fifth Amendment's Due Process Clause because it did not deprive citizens of the liberty of contract without due process.
(2) This case represents a fundamental shift from the Presumption of Liberty to the Presumption of Constitutionality. This is a very important concept. Before *Parrish*, the Court assumed that laws were invalid and required the government to prove that they were valid. Now, the Court assumes that laws are valid and requires the challenger to prove that they are invalid.

United States v. Carolene Products (1938)

In 1923, Congress banned the shipment of filled milk. Carolene Products Company manufactured a brand of filled milk called "milnut" (it was mixed with coconut) and was indicted under the law. Carolene Products argued that the law violated the Fifth Amendment's Due Process Clause because it deprived them of their property without due process of law.

The Supreme Court upheld the law. It applied the Presumption of Constitutionality – starting from the assumption that the law was valid – and decided that Carolene Products had not been deprived of its property without due process of law.

But that wasn't the most important part of the case. The most important part was actually a footnote: the famous "Footnote Four." (What a nerdy lawyer thing, right?) Footnote Four carried on the shift that began in *Parrish*. It essentially said three things:
(1) The Presumption of Constitutionality is valid, but when a law deals with the Bill of Rights (any of the first eight amendments), we apply the Presumption of Liberty. For example, if the law restricts the freedom of speech, the court should use the Presumption of Liberty.
(2) The Supreme Court's focus shifted. Before Footnote Four, the Court (as you can see from the cases above) had focused on protecting **economic** rights. However, Footnote Four's reference to the Bill of Rights caused the Court to begin focusing much more on **individual** rights.
(3) The Supreme Court hinted that laws dealing with certain minorities in society should be given extra attention. In other words, if the law deals with a minority, we may want to hold it to a higher standard before we allow it to limit individual liberty.

Key Takeaways from United States v. Carolene Products:
(1) The Presumption of Constitutionality is valid, but when a law deals with any of the first eight amendments (the Bill of Rights), we apply the Presumption of Liberty.
(2) The Supreme Court's focus shifted from economic rights to individual rights.
(3) Footnote Four forecasted what the Court would eventually begin to do: elevate certain laws to higher status based on whether they dealt with certain societal minorities.

SUMMING IT ALL UP

(1) The second era of Due Process Clause law dealt primarily with economic issues. It continued *Dred Scott*'s questionable practice of using the Due Process Clause (which only protects fair **process**) to achieve substantive **outcomes** by creating and inserting certain rights into the three prongs of the Due Process Clause (life, liberty, or property).
(2) *Lochner* is a turning point in the story of the Due Process Clause. While *The Slaughterhouse Cases* and *The Civil Rights Cases* held the Fourteenth Amendment to its original purpose – giving former slaves the full rights of citizenship – *Lochner* began using the Due Process Clause to protect all sorts of other rights (kind-of like *Dred Scott*). In *Lochner*, that right happened to be a previously undiscovered "liberty of contract."

(3) The cases in the second era of Due Process Clause law reveal a massive shift in the Court's view of government. Before this era, the Supreme Court applied the **Presumption of Liberty** to laws that regulated private conduct. This presumption assumed that such laws were invalid and that the government had to prove why they were valid. *Lochner* and *Adkins* are examples of the Presumption of Liberty in action. During and after this era, however, the Supreme Court began to apply the **Presumption of Constitutionality**. This presumption assumed that laws restricting individual liberty were valid and that the challenger had to prove why they were invalid. *Parrish* and *Carolene Products* are examples of the Presumption of Constitutionality in action. You can probably see how the Presumption of Constitutionality is a direct result of *Parrish*'s assumption that the government is allowed to regulate private conduct.

(4) *Carolene Products* Footnote Four created a constitutional tidal wave. It said three things:

(1) When a law deals with the Bill of Rights, the Court applies the Presumption of Liberty (not the Presumption of Constitutionality).

(2) The Supreme Court's focus shifted from economic rights to individual rights.

(3) The Court hinted that laws dealing with societal minorities would be held to a higher standard.

THINGS TO THINK ABOUT

(1) Is the Presumption of Constitutionality a good idea? Some people prefer the Presumption of Constitutionality because it gives the government more freedom to step in and solve what it believes are societal problems. Many others prefer the Presumption of Liberty because it focuses more on protecting individual liberties and limits the government's power over citizens. What do you think? Is it OK for the government to interfere with individual liberty as long as it is to solve a problem in society? At what point is that not OK?

(2) Footnote Four forecasted what the Court would eventually begin to do: elevate certain laws to higher status based on whether they dealt with certain societal minorities. But wait – doesn't the Constitution provide for equal protection of the laws (Chapter 29)? Doesn't it protect the privileges and immunities of citizenship for all Americans (Chapter 28)? Why, then, did the Court feel that this part of Footnote Four was necessary?

(3) Is Footnote Four's elevation of minorities to a higher status in the Court's eyes problematic for the separation of powers? In saying this, the Court was essentially saying that whenever the political process did not reach the "right" result, the Court would ride to the rescue. But – as you'll remember from Chapter 2 – that isn't the Court's job. The Supreme Court doesn't make laws. Congress does.

CHAPTER 27: DUE PROCESS – SEX, PRIVACY, AND "SUBSTANTIVE" DUE PROCESS

We now know that there are two due process clauses in the Constitution. And we've seen a couple of signs that the Due Process Clauses were morphing into something other than what they were originally meant to be. Remember, the whole idea of due process is that it guarantees a certain process – a procedure, or a set of steps that the court will use when it is deciding the case. It doesn't guarantee any particular outcomes or results. Over time, though, the Supreme Court began to use the Due Process Clause for more than the protection of fair process.

This trend created a theory that the Supreme Court has now been using for many years. That theory is called **Substantive Due Process**. This theory involves a 3-step formula:

- First, the Court creates a right and characterizes the right at issue as "fundamental" or "deeply rooted" in American history and tradition.
- Second, the Court inserts that newly-created right into one of the three prongs of the Due Process Clause (life, liberty, or property).

- Third, the Court then reasons that taking away that right would be a deprivation of due process.

Substantive Due Process has been used to create all kinds of rights: the right to work, the right to marry, the right to raise one's children, the right to privacy, and much more. None of these rights are in the Constitution. None of them have ever been approved by your elected legislators.

This chapter examines the development of Substantive Due Process into the modern era and how the Supreme Court used it to create all kinds of very controversial rights.

Bolling v. Sharpe (1954)
Many of Washington, D.C.'s public schools were racially segregated during the 1950s. A group of parents challenged segregation as unconstitutional.

The Supreme Court held that segregated schools were unconstitutional, but it didn't use the avenue you might think (like maybe the Fourteenth Amendment's Equal Protection Clause, which was passed to ensure equal application of the laws). The Court used the Fifth Amendment's Due Process Clause, which guarantees due process before one's liberty can be taken away. The Court reasoned that this clause *also* guaranteed racial equality in public schools. In other words, segregated public schools denied black Americans the "due process" they deserve under the Fifth Amendment.

Key Takeaways from Bolling v. Sharpe:
(1) The Fifth Amendment's Due Process Clause guarantees not only due process but also racial equality in public schools.

Poe v. Ullman (1961)
The state of Connecticut had a spottily enforced law prohibiting the use of birth control. Paul and Pauline Poe were charged with violating the law. They argued that the law violated the Due Process Clause of the Fourteenth Amendment.

The Supreme Court dismissed the case because it did not present a clear question for the Court to answer. However, the important part of the case was Justice Harlan's dissent from the dismissal.

Justice Harlan wrote that, in his view, due process was not about process at all. For Harlan, it was a way for judges to invalidate statutes they thought were wrong. He then characterized the Fourteenth Amendment's Due Process Clause as including a broad, undefined range of rights that had yet to be discovered. He argued that one of these undiscovered rights was the right of "privacy of the home." Where did he find this right? We're not sure, because he made it up. Justice Harlan felt that that the "privacy of the home" was part of the "liberty" prong of the Due Process Clause. Therefore, taking away the privacy of the home without due process of law violated the Due Process Clause.

Key Takeaways from Poe v. Ullman:
(1) This was the first appearance of the concept of "privacy of the home." It was invented by Justice Harlan using Substantive Due Process theory.
(2) Notice how Justice Harlan's dissent echoes the dissenting opinion in *The Slaughterhouse Cases*, which predicted that the Fourteenth Amendment would become a fount of undiscovered rights.

Griswold v. Connecticut (1965) (*"the birth control case"*)
The state of Connecticut banned the use of birth control. In 1961, the Connecticut Birth Control League, led by Estelle Griswold, opened a Planned Parenthood clinic in New Haven. Griswold challenged the Connecticut law in court.

The Supreme Court held that the Connecticut ban was unconstitutional. Citing Justice Harlan's privacy concept from *Poe v. Ullman*, the Court based its decision on a "right of marital privacy." However, rather than rooting that right in the Fourteenth Amendment's Due Process Clause like Justice Harlan did in *Poe*, the Court located it in the several amendments that make up the Bill of Rights (the first 8 amendments).

To explain how the Bill of Rights contained the same "privacy" right that Justice Harlan had discovered in the Fourteenth Amendment's Due Process Clause, the Court wrote that the amendments in the Bill of Rights have "penumbras," or "zones," that surround them. These "penumbras" are formed by "emanations" from the Bill of Rights. (Emanations are rays of light). It was in these ethereal "emanations" from the imaginary "penumbras" of the Bill of Rights that the right of privacy was located. In other words, the Bill of Rights had two levels of imaginary abstraction from which the Court pulled a "right of privacy." Despite not being in the Constitution, this right of privacy – which the Court said was "older than the Bill of Rights" – apparently prevented states from banning contraception use.

If this seems strange to you, you're not alone. Penumbras? Imaginary rays of light coming out of the Bill of Rights? Is this in any way related to constitutional law?

Justice Harlan wrote a concurring opinion (an opinion that agrees with the holding in the case) arguing the same thing he had argued in *Poe v. Ullman*: that the right of privacy did not come from the "emanations" of the "penumbras" of the Bill of Rights but instead was part of the liberty protected by the Due Process Clause. Justice Harlan was essentially arguing for a use of Substantive Due Process to create the right of privacy. It wasn't long before his opinion became the dominant viewpoint.

Key Takeaways from Griswold v. Connecticut:
(1) The "right of marital privacy" prevents states from banning the use of birth control.
(2) *Griswold* is a direct result of *Poe v. Ullman*. It isn't too far of a leap from "privacy of the home" to "marital privacy."
(3) *Griswold* is the fulfillment of Footnote Four! One of Footnote Four's impacts was to shift the Court's focus from economic rights to individual rights. *Griswold* is the perfect example of that. No longer was the Court worried about the liberty of contract; now, it was focused on the privacy and intimacy of the marital relationship.
(4) Notice how *Griswold* bucks the trend of using the Presumption of Constitutionality. The Court assumed the law was invalid. Why the sudden change?

Roe v. Wade (1973) ("*the abortion case*")

Texas had a law prohibiting abortions. Jane Roe (whose real name was Norma McCarvey) filed a lawsuit claiming that the law was unconstitutional. She argued that the law abridged her personal "right of privacy" (remember *Poe* and *Griswold*?) which was protected by the Due Process Clause of the Fourteenth Amendment.

Using the now-familiar Substantive Due Process theory framework, the Supreme Court held that the "liberty" portion of the Due Process Clause included a "right of privacy," and that "right to privacy" includes the right to have an abortion. Therefore, taking away the right to have an abortion was essentially taking away liberty without the due process of law. The Court offered no support for this conclusion other than a brief citation to *Buck v. Bell*, a case that upheld the forced sterilization of mentally impaired women.

Key Takeaways from Roe v. Wade:
(1) The "liberty" portion of the Due Process Clause included a "right of privacy," and that "right to privacy" includes the right to have an abortion. Therefore, taking away the right to have an abortion was essentially taking away liberty without the due process of law.
(2) *Roe* was the fulfillment of Justice Harlan's *Poe* and *Griswold* opinions. Harlan wrote that the right of privacy did not come from the "emanations" of the "penumbras" of the Bill of Rights. Instead, it was part of the liberty protected by the Due Process Clause. The *Roe* Court adopted this view when it used Substantive Due Process theory to create a right to abortion.

Lawrence v. Texas (2003)

A Texas law prohibited intimate sexual conduct between two persons of the same sex. John Lawrence and Tyron Garner were convicted under this law. They challenged their convictions. The Supreme Court held that the Texas law was invalid because it violated the right of sexual privacy found within the Due Process Clause of the Fourteenth Amendment.

Key Takeaways from Lawrence v. Texas:

(1) A Texas law prohibiting intimate sexual conduct between two persons of the same sex violated the right of sexual privacy found within the Due Process Clause of the Fourteenth Amendment.

Obergefell v. Hodges (2015) (*"the gay marriage case"*)

Ohio, Michigan, and Kentucky banned same-sex marriage. Same-sex couples challenged these laws, arguing that they violated the Due Process Clause of the Fourteenth Amendment.

The Supreme Court held that the Due Process Clause of the Fourteenth Amendment protects the right to marry as a fundamental liberty for same-sex couples. The Court's reasoning followed a now-familiar Substantive Due Process formula: (1) create a new right and say that it is "fundamental," (2) include the right in one of the prongs of the Due Process Clause (which provides due process before you can be deprived of "life, liberty, or property"), then (3) reason that taking away that right would result in a deprivation of due process.

Key Takeaways from Obergefell v. Hodges:
(1) The Due Process Clause of the Fourteenth Amendment protects the right to marry as a fundamental liberty for same-sex couples.

Planned Parenthood of Pennsylvania v. Casey (1992)

Pennsylvania's abortion control law required a 24-hour waiting period prior to the procedure. It also required minors to get the consent of 1 parent and women to get the consent of their husbands before proceeding with the abortion. Planned Parenthood challenged the law.

The Supreme Court upheld every requirement except the husband-consent requirement. It created a new standard for abortion cases which asks whether an abortion regulation has the purpose or effect of imposing an "undue burden" on a woman seeking an abortion.

Justice Kennedy, who wrote the majority opinion, did not use the typical Substantive Due Process framework. Instead, he based his conclusion on the statement that "[a]t the heart of liberty is the right to define one's own concept of existence, of meaning, of the universe, and of the mystery of human life."

No one has any idea what that means or how it supports the conclusion in the case, but it sounds nice.

<u>Key Takeaway from Planned Parenthood of Pennsylvania v. Casey</u>:
(1) An abortion regulation that imposes an "undue burden" on a woman seeking an abortion is invalid.

SUMMING IT ALL UP

(1) The Supreme Court held in *Bolling v. Sharpe* that the Fifth Amendment's Due Process Clause guarantees not only due process but *also* racial equality in public schools.
(2) The "right of privacy" does not come from the Constitution. It was first mentioned in Justice Harlan's dissent from the Supreme Court's dismissal of *Poe v. Ullman*. Harlan said that it came from the Fourteenth Amendment's Due Process Clause, but the Court later said in *Griswold that* it came from the "emanations" of the "penumbras" of the Bill of Rights (the first eight amendments). Which is it? And what on earth are the "emanations" of the "penumbras" of the Bill of Rights? *Roe v. Wade* held that the "liberty" portion of the Due Process Clause included a "right of privacy," and that "right to privacy" includes the right to have an abortion. Therefore, taking away the right to have an abortion was essentially taking away liberty without the due process of law.
(4) After *Casey*, an abortion regulation that imposes an "undue burden" on a woman seeking an abortion is invalid. We aren't entirely sure what an "undue burden" is.
(5) You can see the expansion of the notion of privacy in these cases. From *Poe v. Ullman* to *Griswold* to *Roe* to *Lawrence*, the Supreme Court went from privacy of the home to marital privacy to sexual privacy. Talk about living up to Footnote Four's focus on individual rights! However, there are concerns that come along with this shift. The privacy concept relied on by the Court in all of these cases does not exist anywhere in the Constitution, nor was it voted in by our elected representatives. It was created by the Court – and they can't even agree on where it supposedly comes from! In light of what we learned about the judiciary in Chapter 7, is this OK?

(6) Justice Field's dissent in *The Slaughterhouse Cases* (Chapter 25) argued that the Fourteenth Amendment protected much more than just the equality of former slaves. The cases in this chapter show how his opinion has now become the majority view. On multiple occasions, the Court has now used Substantive Due Process to create rights out of the Fourteenth Amendment.

THINGS TO THINK ABOUT

(1) Is Substantive Due Process a valid theory? Think of a NASCAR racing track. There are rails or sides on a racetrack that the cars must stay within. If they go outside the racetrack, they are disqualified. The rails exist to make sure that everyone has to race on the same track based on the same standards. Do the rails also determine who the winner of the race is? Of course not. They are just there to ensure that all the competitors go through the same process in order to cross the finish line. How then do we justify Substantive Due Process? How can something that guarantees only process also guarantee particular outcomes? If that's the case, why bother having a Due Process Clause at all? The validity of Substantive Due Process is still debated today. Some believe that the Fourteenth Amendment's Due Process Clause protects substantive rights. Others argue that it "is not a secret repository of substantive guarantees against unfairness." What do you think?

(2) Chief Justice John Roberts has compared *Obergefell* to *Lochner* and *Dred Scott*. He argues that *Obergefell* did the same thing those two cases did: create the result the Court wanted by warping the Due Process Clause into something it fundamentally could not be: a guarantor of favored policy results that were nowhere in the Constitution. Is this comparison legitimate?

(3) These cases also raise questions about federalism. At the time *Roe v. Wade* was decided, 46 states had laws banning abortion. The Court essentially overruled what 46 of the state legislatures had decided. The same was true in *Obergefell*: the majority of the states did not allow same-sex marriage at the time of the decision. Think back to Chapter 2, where we talked about federalism. In a federalist system that divides power between the federal and state governments, can the federal courts overrule the states' validly enacted laws? Does a group of 9 Ivy-League-educated judges overruling 46 elected state legislatures raise any questions about the power of the federal government in relation to the states?

(4) The majority opinion in *Obergefell* was based in part abstract philosophizing about the dignity of humanity. Is there a "right to dignity" in the U.S. Constitution? Should there be? What about the fact that North Korea's Constitution has that right plus dozens of others, including a "right to relaxation"?

CHAPTER 28: PRIVILEGES OR IMMUNITIES

This chapter is about the Privileges or Immunities Clause of the Fourteenth Amendment. As you know, the Fourteenth Amendment was originally passed to protect the civil liberties of former slaves. The Privileges or Immunities Clause helps accomplish this goal by ensuring that states can't make laws that infringe on the "privileges or immunities" of their citizens. This generally means that states cannot deprive their citizens of fundamental rights.

The key question regarding the Privileges or Immunities Clause is, "What are privileges or immunities"? The cases and discussion below will show how the Supreme Court has tried to answer that question.

The Slaughterhouse Cases (1873)

Remember this one?

Louisiana gave a monopoly to a private slaughterhouse called Crescent City Slaughterhouse Company. A group of butchers sued the state, arguing that the monopoly given to Crescent violated (among other things) the Privileges or Immunities Clause of the Fourteenth Amendment.

The Supreme Court held that the monopoly did not violate the Privileges or Immunities Clause of the Fourteenth Amendment. This was because the Fourteenth Amendment was passed with the narrow goal of granting full equality to former slaves. It was not passed to protect any and all rights that a citizen may claim. Holding the monopoly invalid, reasoned the Court, would have led to excessive federal government control of the states. And that would not be acceptable, since the protection of the privileges or immunities of the citizens was for the states to do – not the federal government.

As a result, the Privileges or Immunities Clause came to be seen as only protecting the privileges of federal citizenship. Therefore, *The Slaughterhouse Cases* ruling essentially destroyed the Privileges or Immunities Clause.

SUMMING IT ALL UP

(1) *The Slaughterhouse Cases* held that a state-granted monopoly to a private slaughterhouse did not violate the Fourteenth Amendment's Privileges or Immunities Clause. The protection of the privileges or immunities of the citizens, stated the Court, was for the states to do – not the federal government. This decision severely weakened the Privileges or Immunities Clause.

THINGS TO THINK ABOUT

(1) What are "privileges or immunities"? The short answer: it's up in the air. However, if you look back to Chapter 9's discussion of the Article IV Privileges and Immunities Clause, you'll see that Georgetown law professor Randy Barnett has put forth what may be the most complete analysis so far. He believes that "privileges or immunities" includes (1) fundamental rights belonging to citizens of free governments, (2) those rights that have been consistently upheld throughout the United States' history (life, liberty, property, pursuit of happiness, contracts, purchase, sell, convey, etc.), and the rights enumerated in the Bill of Rights (the first eight amendments).

(2) The Supreme Court essentially killed the Privileges or Immunities Clause in *The Slaughterhouse Cases*. Therefore, in order to compensate for how weak the Privileges or Immunities Clause had become, the Court started using the Due Process Clause to create results. We saw this happen in Chapters 26 & 27. For instance, *Lochner* held that the liberty of contract was a fundamental right protected by the Due Process Clause, even though the Privileges or Immunities Clause would seem to be the more logical place to find that fundamental right. It's worth asking whether the Due Process Clause decisions we've studied should have been decided under the Privileges or Immunities Clause. After all, the Due Process Clause is about *process*, not *substance*. Wouldn't the Privileges or Immunities Clause be the appropriate way to bring claims regarding individual rights?

CHAPTER 29: EQUAL PROTECTION

We are finally at our last chapter on the Fourteenth Amendment.

The Equal Protection Clause says that states cannot deny any citizen the equal protection of the laws. In other words, states can't give only some of their citizens legal protection; they must give legal protection to all citizens.

It is important to say what the Equal Protection Clause does *not* do. It does not require states or the federal government to eliminate every inequality in every circumstance. Inequality is a fact of life. We are all very different and unequal from each other in terms of talents, physical characteristics, interests, and more, and every law creates inequality of some sort. The Equal Protection Clause does not guarantee perfect equality of outcomes. It only guarantees that all citizens will be subject to the same legal standards. In other words, it isn't trying to give all the students in the class the same grade – it's just concerned with making sure they are all graded on the same curve.

The chapter is divided into sections. Each section includes the cases that dealt with a particular topic within the realm of the Equal Protection Clause.

RACE

The Slaughterhouse Cases (1873)

I know, it's starting to get old.

But we have to look at this case one more time. Turns out it was pretty important!

Louisiana gave a monopoly to a private slaughterhouse called Crescent City Livestock Landing and Slaughterhouse Company. A group of butchers sued the state, arguing that the monopoly given to Crescent violated (among other things) the Equal Protection Clause of the Fourteenth Amendment.

The Supreme Court held that the monopoly did *not* violate the Equal Protection Clause of the Fourteenth Amendment. This was because the Fourteenth Amendment was passed with the specific goal of granting full equality to former slaves. It was not passed to protect any and all rights a citizen may claim.

Key Takeaway from The Slaughterhouse Cases:
(1) A state-granted monopoly to a private slaughterhouse did not violate the Fourteenth Amendment's Equal Protection Clause.

Yick Wo v. Hopkins (1886) (*"the laundry case"*)

The city of San Francisco required all launders to get a permit from the city. Nearly 90% of the city's launders were of Chinese descent, but not a single Chinese launder was granted a permit. A launder named Yick Wo was imprisoned after refusing to pay the fine for operating a laundry without a permit. He sued the city, arguing that the city law violated the Equal Protection clause.

The Supreme Court held that the city's actions violated Yick Wo's rights under the Equal Protection clause of the Fourteenth Amendment because the city officials enforced the law unequally against people of Chinese descent.

Key Takeaway from Yick Wo v. Hopkins:
(1) Denying an entire ethnic group a permit that all launders were required to get – even though that group made up 90% of the launders in the city – violated the Equal Protection Clause.

Bolling v. Sharpe (1954)

Remember this one? We talked about it in Chapter 27.

In the 1950s, any of Washington, D.C.'s public schools were racially segregated. After several parents objected to this practice, a lawsuit was filed challenging the segregated schools as unconstitutional.

The Supreme Court held that segregated schools were unconstitutional, but it didn't use the avenue you might think (like maybe the Equal Protection Clause). The Court used the Fifth Amendment's Due Process Clause, which guarantees due process before one's life, liberty, or property can be taken away. The Court reasoned that this clause *also* guaranteed racial equality in public schools. In other words, segregated public schools denied black Americans the "due process" that they deserve under the Fifth Amendment. As we've seen (Chapter 27), this is a typical use of "Substantive" Due Process theory.

But here's the Equal Protection Clause angle. The Court essentially used the Fifth Amendment's Due Process Clause (which applies to the federal government) to guarantee something that the Equal Protection Clause (which applies to the states) already guarantees! The Equal Protection Clause was designed to ensure that states provided equal legal protection to all of their citizens. In *Sharpe*, the Court applied this guarantee to the federal government without saying so, and it used the Fifth Amendment's Due Process Clause – which has nothing to do with equal protection – to do so.

Key Takeaways from Bolling v. Sharpe:
(1) The Fifth Amendment's Due Process Clause guarantees not only due process but *also* racial equality in public schools.
(2) The Court used the Fifth Amendment's Due Process Clause (which applies to the federal government) to guarantee something that the Equal Protection Clause (which applies to the states) already guarantees. In a way, the Court applied the Equal Protection Clause to the federal government.

Brown v. Board of Education (1954)

Black students who were denied admittance to segregated public schools in Kansas, South Carolina, Virginia, Delaware, and Washington, D.C. argued that segregation violated the Equal Protection Clause of the Fourteenth Amendment. The lower courts denied their request on the basis of the "separate but equal" doctrine. This "separate but equal" doctrine came from *Plessy v. Ferguson*, a previous case that upheld segregated railway cars. It was essentially the idea that segregation was acceptable as long as both groups were treated equally.

The Supreme Court held that "separate but equal" public schools violated the Equal Protection Clause of the Fourteenth Amendment.

Key Takeaways from Brown v. Board of Education:
(1) "Separate but equal" public schools violated the Equal Protection Clause of the Fourteenth Amendment.

Loving v. Virginia (1967)

Richard Loving, a white man, and Mildred Jeter, a black woman, were married in the District of Columbia. They moved to Virginia soon after and were charged with violating the state's ban on interracial marriage. They challenged the law as a violation of the Equal Protection Clause.

The Supreme Court held that Virginia's ban on interracial marriage violated the Equal Protection Clause because it's clear purpose was racial discrimination.

Key Takeaway from Loving v. Virginia:
(1) Bans on interracial marriage violate the Equal Protection Clause of the Fourteenth Amendment.

SEX

Frontiero v. Richardson (1973)

Sharron Frontiero, a Lieutenant in the Air Force, requested government benefits for her husband, who was a full-time student. The Air Force denied her request because she failed to demonstrate that her husband was dependent on her for more than half his support. Federal law at the time listed wives of military members as dependents; husbands, however, could not be dependents unless they were dependent on their wife for more than half of their support. The Supreme Court held that this law violated the Equal Protection Clause because it treated two groups of people differently under the law without sufficient justification.

Key Takeaway from Frontiero v. Richardson:
(1) A law that puts additional legal burdens on members of one sex and not the other without sufficient justification violates the Equal Protection Clause.

AFFIRMATIVE ACTION

Regents of the University of California v. Bakke (1978)

The University of California Medical School reserved 16 places out of each class of 100 people for minorities as part of the school's Affirmative Action program. The point of the program was to make up for low numbers of minority students in the past.

Allan Bakke, a 35-year-old white man, had exam scores and GPA levels that exceeded those of every minority student admitted through the Affirmative Action program, but he was nonetheless denied admission. Bakke sued, arguing that the program violated the Equal Protection Clause.

The Supreme Court held that the medical school was required to admit Bakke and that the use of racial quotas in admissions programs violated the Equal Protection Clause. However, it stated that admissions programs could use race as one of many *factors* in the admissions process.

The Court also stated for the first time that achieving "diversity" in education was a legitimate goal for schools to pursue.

Key Takeaways from Regents of the University of California v. Bakke:
(1) The use of racial quotas in admissions programs violates the Equal Protection Clause, but race can be used as one of many *factors* in the admissions process.

Gratz v. Bollinger (2003) & Grutter v. Bollinger (2003) (*"the Michigan cases"*)

These two cases involved Affirmative Action plans at the University of Michigan.

Gratz dealt with a challenge to the undergraduate admissions program, which made race the single most important factor in the admissions process. The Supreme Court found that this policy violated the Equal Protection Clause because it resulted in nearly every minority applicant getting admitted without consideration of their merits.

Grutter dealt with the law school's admissions program, which considered race only as a "plus factor" rather than a core factor in the admissions process. The Supreme Court held that this policy did *not* violate the Equal Protection Clause because race was only one factor among many and it did not cause the law school to abandon a full review of each application.

In both cases, Justice Clarence Thomas – the only black justice on the Court – wrote that Affirmative Action programs are unconstitutional race discrimination programs because they prioritize some people over others based on their race.

Key Takeaway from Gratz v. Bollinger & Grutter v. Bollinger:
(1) If race is the single most important factor in an admissions process, the process violates the Equal Protection Clause. However, if race is a "plus factor," there is no Equal Protection Clause violation.

Fisher v. University of Texas (2016)

The University of Texas developed a policy in which race was one of factors considered in the admissions process. Abigail Fisher sued the university after her application was rejected, arguing that the consideration of race in the admissions process violated the Equal Protection Clause.

The Supreme Court upheld the policy. In other words, the University of Texas' consideration of race in the admissions process did not violate the Equal Protection Clause. This was because the university's pursuit of "diversity" was a valid goal that justified using race to make admissions decisions.

Just like in *Gratz* and *Grutter*, Justice Thomas dissented, arguing that the Equal Protection Clause does not permit the consideration of race in admissions decisions.

Key Takeaway from Fisher v. University of Texas:
(1) The University of Texas' use of race as a factor in the admissions process did not violate the Equal Protection Clause because the university's pursuit of "diversity" was a valid goal that justified using race to make admissions decisions.

PRIVACY & SEXUAL ORIENTATION

Eisenstadt v. Baird (1972)

William Baird gave free birth control to a woman who attended a lecture he gave on using birth control to prevent over-population. The state of Massachusetts charged Baird under a state law that prohibited giving contraceptives to unmarried individuals. Baird challenged the law as a violation of the "right of privacy" that the Court had created in *Griswold v. Connecticut* (Chapter 27).

The Supreme Court held that the Massachusetts law violated the Equal Protection Clause. However, it based its decision on *Griswold*'s "right of privacy," saying that everyone has the right to be "free from governmental intrusion into . . . the decision whether to bear or beget a child."

The "right of privacy" created by the Court in Due Process cases had now been imported into the Equal Protection context. It also had morphed from a right of *marital* privacy to a right of *individual* privacy.

Key Takeaways from Eisenstadt v. Baird:
(1) A law prohibiting unmarried people from using birth control violated the Equal Protection Clause because it intruded on the individual's right of privacy.

United States v. Windsor (2013)

Congress passed the Defense of Marriage Act (DOMA) with broad support from both political parties and President Bill Clinton. Section 3 of the Act defined marriage as being between one man and one woman. Edith Windsor challenged the law as unconstitutional.

The Supreme Court held that DOMA was unconstitutional because it violated – get this – the *Fifth Amendment's* guarantee of *equal protection.* How is this possible? The Fifth Amendment doesn't even have an Equal Protection Clause!

Go back to the beginning of this chapter, to *Bolling v. Sharpe.* In that case, the Supreme Court held that the Fifth Amendment's Due Process Clause guarantees not only due process but *also* racial equality in public schools. The Court essentially used the Fifth Amendment's Due Process Clause (which applies to the federal government) to guarantee something that the Equal Protection Clause (which applies to the states) already guarantees.

This is what makes the decision in *Windsor* possible. Since *Sharpe* had essentially applied the equal protection guarantee to the federal government, the Court could say in *Windsor* that a federal law violated the equal protection of the laws even though the Equal Protection Clause doesn't apply to the federal government.

Key Takeaway from United States v. Windsor:

(1) DOMA was unconstitutional because it violated the Fifth Amendment's guarantee of equal protection. The irony is, of course, that the Fifth Amendment does not guarantee equal protection. The Court was able to reach this conclusion because of *Bolling v. Sharpe.*

VOTING

Reynolds v. Sims (1964) (*"the voting case"*)

The Alabama state constitution required one representative per county. At the same time, some electoral districts had far more voters than others. This put citizens in highly populated counties (such as those containing large cities) at a significant disadvantage when it came to voting because they still only received one representative despite their much larger population. Several citizens argued that Alabama's electoral district plan violated the Equal Protection Clause.

The Supreme Court agreed with them. The Court stated that the Equal Protection Clause requires substantially equal representation for all citizens. Therefore, state district plans should try to achieve equal populations in each electoral district.

Key Takeaways from Reynolds v. Sims:

(1) The Equal Protection Clause requires substantially equal representation for all citizens. Therefore, state district plans should try to achieve equal populations in each electoral district.

SUMMING IT ALL UP

(1) The Equal Protection Clause says that states cannot deny any citizen the equal protection of the laws. It does not require states or the federal government to eliminate every inequality in every

circumstance. It only guarantees that all citizens will be subject to the enforcement of the same legal standards.

(2) Bans on interracial marriage violate the Equal Protection Clause.

(3) A law that puts additional legal burdens on members of one sex and not the other violates the Equal Protection Clause.

(4) The use of rigid racial quotas in admissions programs violates the Equal Protection Clause, but race can be used as one *factor* in the admissions process as part of the quest for greater "diversity."

(5) A law prohibiting unmarried people from using birth control violated the Equal Protection Clause of the Fourteenth Amendment because it intruded on the individual's right of privacy. The "right of privacy" created by the Court in the Due Process Clause cases had now been imported into the Equal Protection context. It also had morphed from a right of *marital* privacy to a right of *individual* privacy.

(6) The Defense of Marriage Act was unconstitutional because it violated the Fifth Amendment's guarantee of equal protection. The irony is, of course, that the Fifth Amendment does not guarantee equal protection. The Court was able to reach this conclusion because *Bolling* v. *Sharpe* used the Fifth Amendment's Due Process Clause (which applies to the federal government) to essentially apply the Equal Protection Clause (which applies to the states) to the federal government.

(7) The Equal Protection Clause requires substantially equal representation for all citizens. Therefore, state district plans should try to achieve equal populations in each electoral district.

THINGS TO THINK ABOUT

(1) We can see that the Court is applying the Presumption of Liberty much more often now. (Remember: the Presumption of Liberty is the assumption that laws restricting liberty are invalid unless the government can prove otherwise). Almost every one of the cases in this chapter describes the Court invalidating a law, not upholding it. Why is that? Is it because the Court is now dealing with individual rights rather than economic rights? Should that make a difference?

(2) In *Bolling* v. *Sharpe*, the Court essentially applied the Equal Protection Clause to the federal government. If Due

Process *includes* Equal Protection, why did Congress write a separate Equal Protection Clause?

(3) The Supreme Court held in *Brown v. Board of Education* that "separate but equal" public schools violated the Equal Protection Clause of the Fourteenth Amendment. The result in *Brown* could just as easily – or perhaps more easily – have been based on the Privileges or Immunities Clause of the Fourteenth Amendment. This is particularly true in light of the fact that nearly every legislator who voted to pass the Fourteenth Amendment believed that public school attendance was a "privilege" of national citizenship. But because the Court destroyed the Privileges or Immunities Clause in *The Slaughterhouse Cases*, that wasn't an option.

(4) What about federalism? Federalism is the division of power between the states and the federal government in which the states are supposed to have the freedom to make their own laws. But *Sims* and *Windsor* seem to contradict that. *Sims* said that the federal government could force the states to change their voting districts, and *Windsor* overruled numerous valid state laws. Is this a problem in light of the Tenth Amendment (see Chapter 21)?

(5) The Constitution only requires that the states have a "republican" form of government (through elected representatives). It says nothing about vote apportionment or electoral population. In light of that, what do we make of *Sims'* requirement of equal representation in electoral districts?

(6) Notice how these cases are the manifestation of Footnote Four's prophecy. Footnote Four predicted that laws dealing with minorities should be highly scrutinized. In the cases above, almost all of which dealt with societal minorities, the Court heavily scrutinized the law and – in almost every instance – struck it down. Footnote Four's prophecy was starting to come true. Is this a good thing? Should certain laws be singled out to meet a higher standard than others? Based on what?

(8) And then there's the Affirmative Action controversy. One side of the debate says that Affirmative Action programs are necessary to correct discrimination that happened in the past; the other side says that Affirmative Action programs are race-based discrimination. What do you think? Why?

(9) The Equal Protection Clause obviously deals with the concept of equality. As we discussed in Chapter 1, the framers drew the American idea of "legal equality before the law" from the Christian moral idea of "moral equality before God." They weren't interested in giving everyone the same income or making sure there were the same number of CEOs in each demographic group; they simply believed that all of us are equal in our possession and pursuit of freedom. Their counterparts on the other side of the Atlantic – the French Revolutionaries – saw things differently. They believed in *absolute* equality and saw *any* differences between people as evidence of evil. Given the murderous failure of the French Revolution, one would think that such ideas would be dismissed as incorrect. However, the American framers' concept of equality is again under attack by those who advocate for absolute equality. A new definition of equality has been created, one that seeks to distribute life outcomes so that everyone has the same results. It goes by the name of "socialism," and it – like the French Revolutionaries – sees any differences between people as wrong. Is this idea of equality a good development or a bad one? Why or why not? Does the comparison between the successful American Revolution and the failed French Revolution help us think about this?

CHAPTER 30: ADMINISTRATIVE LAW

Administrative law is not constitutional law, but it is important to understand because it is wrapped up with constitutional law issues. Administrative law deals with administrative agencies. These are unelected governmental bodies that make rules and regulations that affect our daily lives.

There are two kinds of administrative agencies: (1) executive and (2) independent. Executive agencies work for the Executive Branch (the President). Independent agencies are not under the control of any branch.

Administrative law stems from the ideas of German philosophers who believed that experts – not voters – should run society. They thought that the people were not smart enough to know how to govern, so they recommended replacing democracy with a class of experts who could guide us to the ultimate society. President Woodrow Wilson liked these ideas and imported them into American constitutional law, even though they were directly contrary to the framers' belief in the "consent of the governed." During the New Deal, President Franklin D. Roosevelt built on Wilson's administrative framework and created dozens of new agencies. President Lyndon B. Johnson furthered expanded administrative agencies in his failed Great Society project. Since then, administrative agencies have been an ever-present but largely unrecognized force in American life.

Agencies are incredibly powerful. They can do pretty much anything the federal government can do (and sometimes more). They can write rules and regulations that bind citizens. They have their own courts and judges through which they adjudicate cases. And they can enforce their own regulations. In other words, they have all three powers of government: legislative, executive, and judicial!

Think back to Chapter 2 (I know, it was a long time ago), when we talked about the separation of powers. Why are the powers separated? Because the framers understood that human nature was flawed and that humans would always try to consolidate power in order to gain political advantage. Because they wanted to maximize individual liberty and minimize the dangers of our flawed human nature, they separated the powers of government. Administrative law is thus subject to a constant criticism: that it violates the separation of powers. Administrative agencies combine all three branches of government into a single unelected body that can pretty much do whatever it wants.

GIVING POWER TO ADMINISTRATIVE AGENCIES

The framers made it clear that the separation of powers meant that the three branches of government could not pawn their responsibilities off on each other. In other words, the courts can't just decide they are sick of adjudicating cases and give that job to the President. This idea is called the "non-delegation doctrine" – the idea that the branches cannot *delegate* their jobs away to someone else. This doctrine has been completely abandoned since Congress started giving its legislative power to administrative agencies.

J.W. Hampton, Jr., & Co. v. United States (1928) ("*the delegation case*")

The Tariff Act of 1922 gave the Executive Branch the power to tax imports. The President assigned taxes that caused J.W. Hampton, Jr. & Co. to have to pay high customs fees. The company sued, arguing that Congress could not delegate its law-making power to the Executive branch in this way. In other words, it claimed that the Tariff Act violated the non-delegation doctrine.

The Supreme Court held that Congress did not violate the non-delegation doctrine when it delegated the authority to set tax rates to the Executive. The Court said that Congress could delegate power to another entity as long as there was an "intelligible principle" to guide the use of its power.

Key Takeaways from J.W. Hampton, Jr., & Co. v. United States:
(1) Congress can delegate power to other branches and/or administrative agencies as long as there is an "intelligible principle" to guide the agency's use of its power. What is an "intelligible principle"? We have no idea, and neither does the Court.

J.W. Hampton permanently discarded the non-delegation doctrine (the idea that the branches cannot delegate their jobs away to someone else), which the framers believed was inherent in the separation of powers. The vast majority of cases since then have allowed Congress to give its power to agencies and other branches of government with very few restrictions. After all, a creative judge can find a way to characterize almost anything as an "intelligible principle." The result of this kind of delegation has been a massive shift in power away from the people's elected representatives and toward unelected agencies.

DEFERRING TO ADMINISTRATIVE AGENCIES

The death of the non-delegation doctrine enabled Congress to give its power to agencies.

However, the courts have also begun deferring to agency decisions. In other words, they let the agency's decision override their judgment. The result is that agencies are given power to write laws (delegation) and can then avoid getting challenged when those laws don't work (deference). They gain power on the front end and the back end of the decision-making process. This has led to an even larger reduction in Congressional legitimacy and a continued increase in the power of administrative agencies.

Chevron U.S.A. v. Natural Resources Defense Council (1984) (*"the deference case"*)

The Clean Air Act required states to regulate sources of air pollution (like factories). The Environmental Protection Agency (EPA) passed a regulation allowing states to treat all pollution-emitting sources as a group. For example, rather than regulating every single factory, states could pass one broad regulation that would cover all the factories and save them a lot of time and money. The Natural Resources Defense Council filed suit, arguing that this regulation violated the Clean Air Act.

The Supreme Court held that the regulation did not violate the Clean Air Act. In other words, the EPA's regulation allowing states to group pollution sources together was valid. The Court *deferred* to the EPA's decision because the agency's decision was "reasonable." This decision created a test for determining when courts should defer to an agency's decision. The test states that if the intent of Congress is not clear, the court should defer to the agency's interpretation. The only requirement is that the agency's interpretation must be "reasonable."

Key Takeaways from Chevron U.S.A. Inc. v. Natural Resources Defense Council, Inc.:
(1) The *Chevron* Deference Test: "Is the intent of Congress clear?" If so, then do as Congress says. If not, the court should defer to the agency's "reasonable" interpretation. What is "reasonable"? Good question. No one knows.

SUMMING IT ALL UP

(1) Administrative law has grown tremendously over the years. The decline of the non-delegation doctrine meant that Congress could

delegate its power to administrative agencies, and *Chevron* required courts to defer to agency decisions. Agencies are therefore largely free from accountability on both the front end and back end of the decision-making process.

THINGS TO THINK ABOUT

(1) Defenders of administrative power argue that administrative agencies are **necessary** in a complex society like ours. A large country like the United States must have administrators, they argue, in order to function. What do you think of that argument? Are administrators and bureaucrats necessary for the country to function?

(2) Administrative law is questionably constitutional because they utilize all three powers of government. Does this combination of the three powers make agencies dangerous? Should we be worried about their lack of accountability to the American people, who cannot elect or remove agency officials?

(3) Administrative law has contributed to the gridlock we now see in Congress. When Congress learns that it can escape the hard work of making laws by passing that job off to an agency (through delegation), it will obviously do so. The result is, of course, that Congress itself passes very few laws. Would getting rid of administrative agencies help revitalize Congress?

(4) Administrative law is based on assumptions that are fundamentally different from those that built the American republic. While the American republic is structured on the knowledge that humanity is flawed and that power must be separated in order to restrain human ambition, administrative power is built on the idea that humans actually *can* create the ultimate society and that concentrated power is acceptable as long as it is in the hands of experts. These are fundamentally opposing assumptions.

We can see the growth of this idea throughout American history. The New Deal, for instance, was only possible through a massive expansion of administrative agencies and administrative power. Same with the Great Society. Both of these projects aimed to create the ultimate society through human efforts, a task that required more and more power to be concentrated in the agencies responsible for creating that ultimate society. And the more power we centralized in the federal government, the less freedom we began to have in our individual lives.

Can humans actually create the ultimate society? The leaders of the failed French Revolution thought so. They believed in utopian ideals about human perfectibility and thought they could create the ultimate society once they overthrew the French monarchy. The framers of the American republic, on the other hand, thought that humans could never create the ultimate society and therefore needed a carefully structured government to restrain their inherent flaws. Which set of assumptions is correct?

CONCLUSION

"Freedom is never more than one generation away from extinction. We didn't pass it to our children in the bloodstream. It must be fought for, protected, and handed on for them to do the same, or one day we will spend our sunset years telling our children and our children's children what it was once like in the United States where men were free."
President Ronald Reagan

You made it!

You've covered all the basic constitutional law concepts and cases, and you know where the law stands (or where we think it stands) on most of the primary issues of today. This chapter provides a few closing thoughts on what we've learned.

* * * * *

First things first. Let's review the foundational concepts that were laid out in the Declaration of Independence and detailed in the Constitution. These concepts are the bedrock of our republic:

(1) **Individual Liberty**. The framers were concerned with declaring independence so that each person would be free to pursue their version of the good life. The Constitution put this into action. A

good example is the First Amendment's protection of free speech.

(2) **Equality before the law**. This is the quintessential American ideal, and it is all over the Constitution. The Equal Protection Clause of the Fourteenth Amendment is a good example.

(3) **The Pursuit of Happiness**. The framers knew they couldn't guarantee everyone a perfect life, but they created a government structured to protect the freedom to pursue one's version of what the perfect life is.

(4) **Natural Law.** The Declaration of Independence refers to the "inalienable" rights of humanity, and the Constitution protects those rights. The free exercise of religion, for instance, is a natural right.

(5) **Consent of the Governed**. This is where you come in. The United States is governed by "we the people," which requires the people to be engaged and active in debating and working toward the betterment of the whole. The Constitution absorbs this ideal completely. Take the separation of powers, for instance. The idea behind a separated-powers government was that consolidated power would take away the ability of the people to govern themselves.

* * * * *

We covered the three basic concepts of constitutional law in Chapter 2.

First, federalism is the division of power between the federal government and the states. Remember: the Tenth Amendment says that anything not given to the federal government is reserved for the states. The states get everything else.

Second, within the federal government, power is separated into three branches: legislative, executive, and judicial. They cannot trade responsibilities (this is called the "non-delegation doctrine"). They each have their own realm and their own limitations.

Why does the separation of powers matter? Because of human nature. The framers of the Constitution recognized that humans were flawed, self-interested creatures who would always seek to gain power for themselves. As Alexander Solzhenitsyn wrote, "The line separating good and evil passes not through states, nor between classes, nor between political parties either—but right through every human heart." The framers therefore created a government that worked *against itself* in order to minimize the dangers inherent in human nature. Modern American society is in danger of forgetting this important truth. We would do well to remember that the violent French Revolution stemmed from utopian ideals about human perfection that are the exact opposite of the ideals that underpin the American republic.

Third, the Constitution was created because the Articles of Confederation weren't doing a good enough job of protecting the people and their property.

* * * * *

Let's look at the three branches of government and see if we can identify some trends over time.

First, the judicial branch. It is fair to say that the federal judicial power – the power of the courts – has expanded over time. The framers designed the judiciary as the weakest branch, but today there are nationwide battles over the confirmation of judges. What happened?

"Substantive" Due Process theory is a big part of the answer. Substantive Due Process, you may remember from Chapter 27, is the tool some judges have used to create substantive rights out of the Due Process Clause even though it only protects fair process. They have done this by inserting their preferred right (for example, the right to own slaves in *Dred Scott* or the liberty of contract in *Lochner* or the right of privacy in *Roe v. Wade*) into one of the three prongs of the Due Process Clause (life, liberty, or property), then arguing that taking away that right would be a deprivation of life, liberty, or property without due process. It is a strange twisting of the notion of due process, and it has led to a massive expansion of the judicial power. Think about it: contract liberty for employers, the right to get an abortion, the right to same-sex marriage, and many more controversial topics have been created by judges through the use of Substantive Due Process. Regardless of whether you agree with those particular rights or not, is it a good idea for nine Ivy League-educated lawyers to have that kind of power? If rights can be created by unelected judges, why do we bother electing senators?

Another factor contributing to the expansion of the judicial power is the decline of Originalism and the rise of Living Constitutionalism (see Chapter 7). Living Constitutionalism believes that the Constitution is a living, evolving document that should be updated over time based on society's changing beliefs. Originalism believes that we should look at the text and history in order to understand the original public meaning of the document. The meaning doesn't change – only the application of that meaning to new circumstances does. The growth of a Living Constitutionalist approach has given judges more license to create rights. Some view this as a good thing because it has led to results that modern society tends to agree with. But it's worth asking whether federal judges are better suited than your elected representatives to make societal decisions that affect all of us. A judge's sense of "modern notions of decency," after all, are highly subjective.

* * * * *

Second, the Executive power. It is fair to say that this power has also expanded over time. At first, the Executive was seen as a mere figurehead for the enforcement of the law and the maintenance of foreign relations. Over time, the President came to be seen as more of a "national vision-caster" than a figurehead for enforcement. This is largely a result of President Woodrow Wilson's elitist idea that the Executive should dominate modern government. Now, Presidential elections turn the country upside down every four years with scandals, protests, and even violence. The Executive Branch has more than 4 million employees and controls well over 100 executive agencies. Presidents have been issuing Executive Orders in increasingly large numbers, and one President even said that he planned to go around Congress and create laws on his own! We seem to have forgotten how limited the Executive power really is. More importantly, we've forgotten that the change agent in this country is supposed to be Congress, not the President.

* * * * *

Third, the Legislative power. This branch has changed as well, but it has not been in the same direction as the other two branches. Ironically, the framers feared that the Legislative branch was going to become too powerful. The opposite has happened. The modern Legislative power (i.e., Congress) is now a weak, ineffective version of what it was it was designed to be.

When the Judicial Branch can start making laws through tools like Substantive Due Process, Congress has less to do. When the people learn that the courts can more quickly create their preferred rights, they will turn to the courts rather than go through the legislative process. When the Executive Branch can start making laws through executive orders and administrative agencies, Congress has less responsibility. And when Congress learns that it can pass the hard work of making laws off to administrative agencies that it can blame for any defects in the law, it is of course incentivized to do so. It literally gives its power away. All of these things combine to create a weak and ineffective Congress.

* * * * *

Given the trends described above, it shouldn't surprise us that our country is so polarized over judicial nominations. We no longer trust that our representatives can do anything because we've ceded so much power to people that aren't accountable to us: federal judges and administrative agency experts. The executive can't control them, and the legislature has been giving its power away to them for decades. So the only thing left is for increasingly powerful judges to try to pick up the constitutional pieces.

Hence the polarized battles over the judicial confirmations.

* * * * *

Notice how we've changed our focus. At first, the framers were focused on protecting individual liberty through structures that would allow individuals to pursue their own ends. Today, we are focused on the realization of every individual right we can think of –

all of which are bound up in extremely difficult and contentious moral questions. The result is that the government has gone from overseeing the broad, public aspects of life to overseeing the private, moral aspects of life. It is the fulfillment of Footnote Four's prophecy, and it's worth asking if this change is a good one.

* * * * *

I wrote this book for you, the American citizen.

I did not write it for lawyers or politicians.

I wrote it for everyday Americans who want to understand a little bit more about how to make a difference in their communities on the issues they care about.

I hope this book has made the American system accessible to you. I hope it has helped you understand more fully what it means to be an American citizen. Americans are unbelievably fortunate to live in a free society, and we cannot take it for granted. Many Americans have lost sight of the fact that self-government is a privilege almost unheard of in human history. We've forgotten that we live in the longest continually-operating constitutional republic ever to exist. We fail to see that effective self-governance requires understanding one's government. We ignore the fact that freedom only flourishes where each citizen understands the structures and principles upon which that freedom depends. Freedom doesn't exist on its own; it must be constantly pursued if it is to survive and prosper.

You, however, now understand the wisdom behind the Constitution's structure. Use your new understanding wisely, for it is directly tied to your ability to have a family, work in your job of choice, educate your children as you see fit, worship as you believe, and much more. You owe it to yourselves and your country to know it.

Most of all, I hope this book inspires you to take part in the American story. Because at the end of the day, that's what it is: a story. It is a story of historic ideals toward which we have strived imperfectly but relentlessly. It is a story based on virtue, individual liberty, and equality before the law. It doesn't mandate an outcome for your life, but it protects your ability to pursue happiness. It has faced challenges and overcome them time after time, eventually becoming the world's must successful experiment in freedom. It is the story of a people who have learned from their mistakes and come out stronger than before. This is a story to be proud of and a story to tell our children and our children's children.

Grab ahold of it. It's yours.

Made in the USA
Columbia, SC
23 December 2021

52676818R00070